BECOMING MORE LIKE CHRIST

Becoming More Like Christ

A Daily Prayer Guide to Living the Beatitudes

DAVID E. ROSAGE

CHARIS

SERVANT PUBLICATIONS
ANN ARBOR, MICHIGAN

Charis Books is an imprint of Servant Publications especially designed to serve Roman Catholics.

Servant Publications—Mission Statement
We are dedicated to publishing books that spread the gospel of Jesus Christ, help Christians to live in accordance with that gospel, promote renewal in the church, and bear witness to Christian unity.

Scripture verses, unless otherwise noted, are taken from the Revised Standard Version of the Bible, copyrighted 1946, 1952, 1971 by the Division of Christian Education of the National Council of Churches of Christ in the USA. Used by permission. Scripture verses marked JB are taken from The Jeruselem Bible.

Servant Publications
P.O. Box 8617
Ann Arbor, MI 48107
www.servantpub.com

Cover design: Steve Eames

03 04 05 06 10 9 8 7 6 5 4 3 2 1

Printed in the United States of America
ISBN 1-56955-386-6

Previously printed as:
Follow Me, paperback, 1982, ISBN 0-89283-168-5
Follow Me, hardcover, 1987, ISBN 0-89283-362-9

Library of Congress Cataloging-in-Publication Data
Rosage, David E.
  [Follow me]
  Becoming more like Christ : a daily prayer guide to living the Beatitudes / David E. Rosage.
    p. cm.
Originally published: Follow me. Ann Arbor, Mich. : Servant Books, c1982.
  ISBN 1-56955-386-6 (alk. paper)
  1. Devotional calendars–Catholic Church. 2. Catholic Church–Prayer-books and devotions–English. 3. Beatitudes–Meditations. I. Title.
  BX2182.3.R6484 2003
  242'.2–dc21
                                                        2003004738

To all devoted followers of Jesus who want to walk even more closely with him.

Contents

Daily Steps to Discipleship

W ho do you say that I am?" (Mt 16:15). Jesus put this question squarely to the apostles at Caesarea Philippi. That same question continues to reecho down through the ages. It has lost none of its relevance. On the contrary, it is even more urgent today than when Jesus first proposed it to his apostles.

Jesus wants us to recognize him for what he is and who he is. He does not want us to know him merely with intellectual knowledge, but with heart knowledge, which we can acquire only through prayerful listening. Jesus wants us to come to know him so intimately that we will be impelled to become more like him, to imitate him so closely that we can be identified with him. This is the import of his call: "Come, follow me" (Mk 10:21).

Out of love God called us into existence. He invited us to become members of his family through our baptism. Jesus' call to discipleship is no less gratuitous; but, let it be said, neither is it less worthy of our total response in love.

The Beatitudes are the blueprint which Jesus laid down to guide and form us in our efforts to become more like him. They are indispensable norms for Christian behavior.

We must "put on Christ" if we are to reach the degree of union with him which Jesus desires for us and which will assure us of our eternal beatitude. Jesus warns us that if we do not put his words into practice we are like the "foolish man who built his house upon the sand." We are to build our house—our spiritual edifice—on a rock foundation (see Mt 7:24-26).

Our call to holiness is a personal invitation from Jesus. He challenges us when he says: "You, therefore, must be perfect, as your heavenly Father is perfect" (Mt 5:48). Jesus came to help us become perfect. This is what he means when he says: "I came that they may have life, and have it abundantly" (Jn 10:10). If we are to enjoy the life of Jesus in all its fullness, we must take time out in our busy schedule to keep our focus fixed on him so that we might be receptive to his divine life. This is not a luxury. It is essential.

By his own example Jesus showed us how important it is to take time out for prayer. Even though he had only three short years in which to evangelize the whole world and to set up his kingdom, he regularly set time aside for prayer away from the crowds. He often rose early in the morning or went off alone at night to be in communion with his Father.

Jesus does not ask us to give him our undivided attention all day long. But by his own example he does point out how necessary it is for us to take at least an occasional "breather" away from our everyday activities to rest with him. These moments aside with Jesus need not be lengthy, but ideally they will inflame our hearts with a yearning for more time alone with him.

An oft-repeated excuse for not praying is that we do not have time to pray. It is true that a dozen demands descend upon us constantly, leaving little or no opportunity for a daily visit with our loving Father. When we permit this to happen it is tragic because prayer is the wellspring of the inspiration and motivation, of the peace and joy we need to fulfill the duties of each day.

One of the reasons for presenting the thoughts in the chapters which follow is to encourage us in a simple way to spend some time each day with the Lord. Through the presence of the Lord in his Word and through the power of that Word, we not only come to know *about* Jesus, but more importantly we come to *know* him—as a person, as an intimate friend.

Becoming More Like Christ suggests a method of prayer for those who desire a more personal relationship with the Lord, but think they do not have time for prayer. Here are a few directives:

1. Before retiring at night select a short Scripture passage from those suggested in the following pages. One verse, one phrase, or even one word may be sufficient. Read it slowly and let every word sink into your heart.

Try to relax for a few moments and ponder the message you have just heard. As you listen to God's Word, your attitude must be "Lord, I know you are present here in your Word; what are you saying to me here and now?"

Perhaps you might find it helpful to read the brief thoughts following each scriptural passage. These short comments are not meant to be an exegetical explanation of the text. Rather, they may serve as a source of inspiration to help us enter into a prayer posture of listening and responding in love.

The import of the message will implant itself in your subconscious and remain with you throughout the night. If you wake during the night or when you awaken in the morning, the thought may be uppermost in your mind. Even if it does not penetrate into your consciousness, its formative power is at work in your heart.

2. Reread the passage in the morning and listen at the core of your being to what the Lord may be saying to you. Spend some time reflecting on his Word, or just basking in his presence and being warmed by his love.

3. If a certain thought strikes you, you may want to linger with it for some time. Jotting down an insight or thought in a journal will assist you in growing and maturing in your relationship with the Lord.

4. Throughout the day recall the thought, the inspiration, or the message which seemed to speak to you. Perhaps making a note of a word or phrase on a slip of paper and keeping it in your pocket or displaying it in a strategic spot (where you will see it often during the course of the day) may help you recall the presence of the Lord and his message.

5. On some days you may not have experienced any great insights or illumination from the passage. This is no reason to be discouraged. The Word of the Lord will mold and transform your heart without you even being aware of it. For example, if you are inclined to be impatient, and if the message of Scripture pointed to the patience of Jesus in dealing with his disciples, his enemies, or sinners, you will automatically be more patient that day without realizing it yourself. You may look back on certain failures in patience throughout the day and wonder whether you are being transformed. But you cannot possibly be aware of the number of times you were *more* patient than usual. That is known to God alone. He does not want us to be spiritual accountants.

The second purpose for presenting these particular passages of Scripture is to deepen our awareness of our call into discipleship—our call to walk more closely in the footprints of the Master.

This book is divided into three parts corresponding to the three phases of the Lord's invitation: *Call, Conditioning,* and *Commitment.*

In Part I we hear God calling us to follow him by living a certain lifestyle—his way of life. This is our call to discipleship. There is only one way we can hear and recognize his call, and that is through the prayer of listening.

In Part II Jesus maps out for us the conditioning which is necessary if we are going to become his disciples. Jesus sets forth the steps of conditioning in the eight Beatitudes which he taught us in the Sermon on the Mount. Jesus assures us: "Blessed are you if you do them" (Jn 13:17).

In Part III we are urged to take that all-important step of commitment which, activated and sustained by love, will make us bear fruit in plenty. "He who abides in me, and I in him,... bears much fruit" (Jn 15:5).

Part I
The Call

The Call

Jesus came to call all people to salvation. We are called to transcendence. Our call comes from the God of heaven and earth and reaches us in this terrestrial realm.

The creating love of the Father called us into existence. Impelled by that same boundless love, our Father called us to become members of his family. Through our baptism he adopted us as his sons and daughters, making us temples of the Holy Spirit and sharing his divine life with us.

Jesus calls each one of us personally to follow the way of life he revealed. When we strive to respond to his call we become his disciples.

Our call has a twofold dimension:

A call to discipleship.

A call to prayer in order to know Jesus as a person.

In the following chapters, which comprise the first section of this plan for a life of prayer, his Word will lead us into a better understanding of our personal call.

Prayer for Generosity

Dearest Lord, teach me to be generous,
teach me to serve you as you deserve:
— to give and not to count the cost,
— to fight and not to heed the wounds,
— to labor and not to ask for reward except that of
knowing I am doing your will. Amen.

(Attributed to St. Ignatius of Loyola)

To Discipleship

If any one hears my voice and opens the door, I will come in to him and eat with him, and he with me.

REVELATION 3:20

A disciple of Jesus is a person who is trying to respond to the personal invitation of Jesus to be his friend and follower. Jesus first encourages us to "come and see" who he is and what he stands for. Then he asks for a deeper commitment: "Come, follow me."

A disciple strives to be like Jesus, to imitate him, to enter into a sympathetic understanding with him so that he can eventually be identified with him.

This relationship with Jesus must be internal rather than merely external. It is introspective rather than extroverted. In the following suggested scriptural passages for each day, let us prayerfully listen to Jesus calling us personally and individually into discipleship.

1 *"Come, follow me."* (Mk 10:21)

Jesus invites me to come and follow him, to become his disciple. He asks me not only to walk in his footsteps, but to follow his way of life so closely that I can be identified with him.

Then my very lifestyle will give witness to his abiding presence in me and in the world.

Jesus, I reach out with joy to grasp your hand so that I may walk more readily in your ways.

2 *"You are my friends if you do what I command you."* (Jn 15:14)

The word for friend in Greek is *philos*—a loved one. Jesus calls me his loved one. If I really love Jesus I will want to do whatever pleases him.

The more I strive to please him, the more closely will I walk in his footsteps. Eventually I will walk so closely to him that I can be identified with him. That is what it means to be a disciple.

Jesus, hasten that day when I hear you calling me "friend."

3 *"I have not come to call the righteous, but sinners to repentance."* (Lk 5:32)

When I hear Jesus inviting me to follow him I shudder at all my weaknesses and my many inadequacies, the mountain of my sinfulness.

However, as I listen to his call once again at the very core of my being, I hear Jesus saying that this is precisely why he called me. He came to forgive, heal, and redeem me. In this redemptive process Jesus enables me to grow in love for him, which is my prime motive in responding to his call to discipleship.

4 *And he said to all, "If any man would come after me, let him deny himself and take up his cross daily and follow me."* (Lk 9:23)

Jesus emphasizes that I must take up my cross each day. My cross is the various demands and duties of each day. Their never-ending recurrence causes them to become routine and monotonous.

However, *what* I do in life is not nearly as important as *why* I perform my daily duties.

Most of the saints did not accomplish extraordinary things, but they did do the ordinary things in an extraordinary manner.

5 *"Come and see."* (Jn 1:39)

Jesus invites me not only to come and see him, but to spend time with him in prayer, to live with him, to strive to capture his way of thinking until "in him we live and move and have our being" (Acts 17:28).

Only after I have "put on the new nature" (Eph 4:24) will I be able to radiate him to all those around me.

Jesus, let me rest often and at length in your presence.

6 *"I am the vine, you are the branches. He who abides in me, and I in him, he it is that bears much fruit, for apart from me you can do nothing."* (Jn 15:5)

With this simple allegory Jesus explained the mystery of his indwelling. He lets the branch blossom out and bear fruit. Yet there would be no fruit if he were not the source of divine life energizing me. How good Jesus is to me!

He reminds me that apart from him I can do nothing, which is another way of saying that with him I can do all things.

7 *"By this my Father is glorified, that you bear much fruit, and so prove to be my disciples."* (Jn 15:8)

Even though Jesus said that without him I could accomplish nothing, nevertheless, supported and strengthened, energized and sustained by his divine life within me, I can give glory to my Father by my feeble efforts to bear fruit.

Just my wanting to be a disciple of Jesus gives glory to God, who accepts my desire as though it were an accomplished fact.

How good God is to me! How wonderful and mysterious is his love for me!

8 *"He who does not take his cross and follow me is not worthy of me."* (Mt 10:38)

When Jesus sends me a cross, he takes into account my strength, my generosity, my willingness to accept a cross.

My cross may simply be striving to live the gospel message.

It may be accepting sickness, old age, some form of handicap, or bearing with another person who tries my patience. It may be some criticism or misunderstanding.

With Jesus let me say: "Father ... not my will, but thine, be done (Lk 22:42).

9 *"Come, I will send you to Pharaoh that you may bring forth my people, the sons of Israel, out of Egypt."* (Ex 3:10)

Humanly speaking, Moses was an unlikely person to be called to lead the Israelites out of Egypt. There was a price on his head in Egypt; he was in exile. Yet God's ways are not our ways.

How unqualified I am for the mission to which the Lord has called me! Jesus reminds me that he chose me; I did not choose him (see Jn 15:16).

Just as he said to Moses, so also the Lord is saying to me: "I will be with you" (Ex 3:12).

10 *"You did not choose me, but I chose you and appointed you that you should go and bear fruit."* (Jn 15:16)

What a privileged person I am! God chose me to be a member of his family, to be his disciple, to be on his team, and also to be an instrument through which his love radiates itself to others. He is asking me to be a channel whereby he can touch others.

I bear fruit when I permit him to transform me and let his radiance shine forth through me.

11 *"Let your light so shine before men, that they may see your good works and give glory to your Father who is in heaven."*
(Mt 5:16)

I need not be concerned about accomplishing any good for others to see. Goodness cannot be hidden. It will radiate and be recognized. This is the light Jesus encouraged me to let shine among men.

God alone is good and whatever goodness shines forth in my attitudes and actions is but a faint reflection of the love with which he fills me.

This is how I can give praise to God.

12 *Then Jesus told his disciples, "If any man would come after me, let him deny himself and take up his cross and follow me."*
(Mt 16:24)

Jesus did not trick me into following him. He spelled out the conditions very clearly.

He challenges me to respond in love to the boundless love which he has for me—this is the price of discipleship.

My daily dying-to-self makes me more open to receive an even greater influx of his enduring love.

Bantu proverb: "The burden of love is light like a cloud."

13 *"Follow me, and I will make you fishers of men."* (Mt 4:19)

Who is who? The almighty, eternal, infinite Creator of the universe wants me to establish a personal union with him so that I can become a channel through which he can touch others with his compassionate, merciful love. As I grow and mature in my relationship with him, I can radiate his peace and joy to others.

What condescension on God's part! How privileged, but how inadequate I am! All I can say is: Here I am, Lord, "I have come to do thy will" (Heb 10:9).

14 *"If any one thirst, let him come to me and drink. He who believes in me ... 'Out of his heart shall flow rivers of living water.'"* (Jn 7:37-38)

When Jesus invites me to come and drink at the source of living water, he is inviting me to be his disciple. He longs to fill me with his life-giving water. All I have to do is let him. He wants me to be magnanimous, to love not only my friends, but even those who make life difficult. Then his love may flow through me and warm others. In short, I am to be a fountain of "living water."

Jesus, keep my heart open, receptive, and ever expansive to the stream of your boundless love.

15 *"I have called you friends, for all that I have heard from my Father I have made known to you."* (Jn 15:15)

Since I am striving to be a disciple of Jesus, he reveals everything to me. Especially does Jesus reveal to me how much his Father loves me and how much he himself loves me.

As my friendship with Jesus deepens I can share all my feelings, my joys and sorrows, my hopes and ambitions, my faults and failures with him, knowing that he will not only accept me as I am, but will support me through thick and thin.

16 *"He who conquers shall have this heritage, and I will be his God and he shall be my son."* (Rv 21:7)

Jesus promises me that if I persevere in being his disciple and following him, I shall gain the victory—which is my eternal union with him in heaven. This victory is symbolized by the morning star shining brightly.

Already I am his adopted son or daughter and he is always my God.

May I always follow the light of the Morning Star and bask in its brilliance!

17 *"Greater love has no man than this, that a man lay down his life for his friends."* (Jn 15:13)

These were not idle words for Jesus. The very next day, he did lay down his life for me.

By trying to respond to his fathomless love for me, I will become his disciple and I will be his friend.

Could I ask for a greater, more loving friend?

18 *[God] saved us and called us with a holy calling, not in virtue of our works but in virtue of his own purpose and the grace which he gave us in Christ Jesus.* (2 Tm 1:9)

I am special to Jesus. He loves me so much he called me to be his disciple, to be closely united with him. In his love he supplies me with all the graces and gifts, the help and encouragement I need to follow his way of life.

I cannot earn heaven. All I can do is to be receptive to his compassionate mercy and respond in loving service.

What I *do* in life is not very important to Jesus, but rather what I *am*. Not *what* I do, but *why* I do it.

19 *"I came not to call the righteous, but sinners."* (Mt 9:13)

Jesus always seems to be more at home with sinners and tax collectors than with the self-righteous. Jesus calls both saints and sinners to fulfill his divine plan.

This truth makes me more comfortable in my call to be a disciple of Jesus. Jesus does not ask me to be perfect before he calls me, but he calls me so that I can grow and mature in holiness. He only asks me to put forth my best efforts and not to count my successes or failures.

20 *"Every one to whom much is given, of him will much be required; and of him to whom men commit much they will demand the more."* (Lk 12:48)

God has gifted me in countless different ways—spiritually, psychologically, and physically. He has done so because he loves me and love must give.

The Lord has endowed me with these many gifts not merely for myself but that I may share and use them to manifest my love for others.

My Father cannot be outdone in generosity. As I give to others, he fills my own heart with much joy.

21 *I therefore, a prisoner for the Lord, beg you to lead a life worthy of the calling to which you have been called, with all lowliness and meekness, with patience, forbearing one another in love.*

(Eph 4:1-2)

Jesus said that when I manifest my love for others all will know that I am his disciple. In his Letter to the Ephesians St. Paul lays down some specifics.

Jesus was humble even in the face of rejection. He was patient with everyone, even with his enemies. He was deeply concerned about the poor and the suffering.

With this image of Jesus before me, and St. Paul's prayerful urging, let me daily take some faltering steps toward this goal.

22 *"Whoever does not bear his own cross and come after me, cannot be my disciple."* (Lk 14:27)

Jesus says to me: "Do not look for a cross. When one comes your way, accept it graciously, cheerfully, willingly, and even gratefully. When I send you a cross it is a sign that I have chosen you to help me carry my cross.

"If you rebel, do not become discouraged. I understand your natural aversion to difficulties and suffering. Try to recall the great love I had for you in accepting my cross. This thought will lighten the burden of your cross."

23 *The gifts and the call of God are irrevocable.* (Rom 11:29)

What a magnificent gift God gave me when he called me to

be his adopted child through my baptism! Jesus reiterated that call when he invited me to be his follower, his disciple.

At times my life does not reflect the dignity of my vocation. I may even get sidetracked in pursuing my vocation. Yet how comforting it is to know that he will always be there to welcome me back.

Thank you, Lord, for your enduring love.

24 *"I am the way, and the truth, and the life; no one comes to the Father, but by me."* (Jn 14:6)

Like space travel, my journey through life is a launch into the unknown. I do not know what tomorrow will bring. However, I do not travel alone; Jesus is my Navigator, for he is *the way.*

If my sights are always on Jesus, *the way,* if my every decision is made in the light of his abiding presence, then I know my journey will bring me home safely into my Father's house.

25 *"Unless a grain of wheat falls into the earth and dies, it remains alone; but if it dies, it bears much fruit."* (Jn 12:24)

Unless I die to myself, my life will remain dormant like the grain of wheat. However, the more I die to my self-centeredness, the more receptive I will be to the influx of God's divine life, which transforms me into his image, and the greater will be the harvest I produce.

Jesus, help me to remember the potential in the grain of wheat.

26 *"He who follows me will not walk in darkness, but will have the light of life."* (Jn 8:12)

Jesus is the beacon of my journey through life. When fears and doubts, misunderstandings and rejections tend to darken my path, I can always depend on Jesus, my guiding Light.

At times he guides me gently, like the reflectors along the highway. At other times a low-beam headlight will amply illumine the way. On still other occasions I may need the high beams to give me a more cosmic vision.

Be that as it may, no follower of Jesus will ever walk in darkness. Thank you, Lord.

27 *[Jesus] said to him, "Follow me." And [Levi] left everything, and rose and followed him.* (Lk 5:27-28)

As a tax collector Levi was hated and despised. He was an outcast, yet Jesus called him to be his disciple.

Jesus likewise calls me, not because I deserve it or because I am qualified. Jesus calls me simply because he loves me, and that love will never leave me as I respond to his call to discipleship.

My RSVP: Thank you for the invitation. Yes, I will try with all my heart to be a loyal disciple.

28 *Christ also suffered for you, leaving you an example, that you should follow in his steps.* (1 Pt 2:21)

Jesus, as you know, I have my favorite crucifix prominently displayed in my room. If I am tempted to indulge in self-pity, a casual glance at your image is a surefire remedy.

When I am angry, offended, discouraged, lonely, or tired, a contemplative gaze at the outpouring of your love on that cross lifts my spirits to new heights.

Thank you for being there, Jesus. Thank you for reminding me of the total gift of your love.

29 *How beautiful upon the mountains are the feet of him who brings good tidings, who publishes peace, who brings good tidings of good, who publishes salvation.* (Is 52:7)

By striving to live very close to Jesus in mind and heart, I bring glad tidings and peace to many hearts.

As I try to keep myself experientially aware of Jesus' abiding presence with me and within me, all my actions and attitudes will reflect the good news of salvation.

I am reminded that actions speak louder than words.

30 *[God] chose us in him before the foundation of the world, that we should be holy and blameless before him.* (Eph 1:4)

I stand in awe and wonder at the mystery of God's goodness and love. I am called to be blameless in his sight so that he can fill me with his love. He wants me to be a happy person.

As I experience the joy, the warmth, the peace and happiness which his love brings me, I will spontaneously reflect his love, peace, and joy to all those I encounter each day.

Lord, may I be a beacon brightly shining in a polluted atmosphere.

31

"If you continue in my word, you are truly my disciples, and you will know the truth, and the truth will make you free."

(Jn 8:31-32)

Jesus' teaching is the word of the Father. That Word has the power to transform me if I listen to it at the very core of my being.

When his Word finds a home in my heart, I will be not only his disciple, but I will experience a freedom, a serenity, a tranquility which the world cannot give me.

What more could a disciple ask?

To Prayer

Lord, teach us to pray.

Luke 11:1

In prayer we establish our personal relationship with the Triune God—the Father who created us, the Son who redeemed us, and the Holy Spirit who sanctifies us.

Prayer is primarily listening. It follows from this simple formula: we cannot know a person to whom we have not listened, nor can we love a person we do not know.

When we strive to listen to God, only then can we know him and that heart knowledge is the wellspring of love.

May the brief words of Scripture on the following pages lead us into a peaceful prayer posture.

1 *"Lord, teach us to pray."* (Lk 11:1)

Prayer is my relationship to God. My prayer is Trinitarian.

Jesus says: "No one can come to me unless the Father who sent me draws him" (Jn 6:44). "No one comes to the Father but by me" (Jn 14:6). "No one can say: 'Jesus is Lord,' except by the Holy Spirit" (1 Cor 12:3).

I augment my relationship with the Father, Son, and Holy Spirit when I pray: "In the name of the Father and of the Son and of the Holy Spirit." and "Glory be to the Father and to the Son and to the Holy Spirit."

2 *Likewise the Spirit helps us in our weakness; for we do not know how to pray as we ought, but the Spirit himself intercedes for us with sighs too deep for words.* (Rom 8:26)

There is a twofold gift in prayer. I must give myself to the Lord in prayer by taking the time and making the effort to be with him.

What happens to me in prayer is the gift of the Holy Spirit operative within me. He is the source of love. In prayer he continues to fill me with his love to the degree that I am willing to surrender myself to him.

Lord, please accept the gift of myself with all my wanderings, distractions, and preoccupations. That is all I have to give.

3 *"If you ask anything in my name, I will do it."* (Jn 14:14)

Jesus wants me to ask so that I will recognize more readily my total dependence on him.

How plainly he said: "Apart from me, you can do nothing" (Jn 15:5).

It is only when the apostles recognized their inability to feed the multitude with five barley loaves and a few dried fish, that Jesus came to their rescue.

Jesus wants me to recognize my helplessness without him so that I may learn to come to him first for help. How appropriate the motto: "Fear not, you are inadequate."

4 *"Come away by yourselves to a lonely place, and rest a while."* (Mk 6:31)

With this invitation, Jesus is teaching me how to handle the busyness of life. He invites me to come by myself to meet him alone in prayer. Here together we can determine what should occupy a high priority on my list and what is of lesser importance.

Only in prayer can I internalize and integrate all those things which are essential to my spiritual growth and which will help me become a committed disciple.

With St. Paul I can forfeit everything else and count it as rubbish so that Christ may be my wealth (see Phil 3:8).

5 *In the morning, a great while before day, he rose and went out to a lonely place, and there he prayed.* (Mk 1:35)

Jesus teaches me how to pray. On this occasion there are no words of Jesus' prayer recorded, but "he was absorbed in prayer." He was united with the Father and the Holy Spirit in a perfect union of love.

My prayer is also simply "being" for God and letting him "be" for me. I am praying when I am resting and relaxing in his presence, letting him love me.

Jesus, help me rise early in the morning like you, or find some other time to be with you in prayer. I know that you are waiting for me.

6 *"Whenever you stand praying, forgive, if you have anything against any one; so that your Father also who is in heaven may forgive you your trespasses."* (Mk 11:25)

Repeatedly Jesus reminds me how necessary it is for me to forgive before I can establish and maintain a deep, personal relationship with my Father in heaven.

If I am nursing some grievance, or indulging in self-pity, or harboring wounded pride, my heart is not free to receive God's love, nor can my love touch others.

Jesus, teach me to pray with you: "Father, forgive them; for they know not what they do" (Lk 23:34).

7 *As he was praying, the appearance of his countenance was altered, and his raiment became dazzling white.* (Lk 9:29)

When Jesus encountered his Father in prayer, a great transformation took place. His divinity radiated through his human body.

St. Paul assures me that when I spend time gazing on the Lord's radiance, I will likewise be transformed and will reflect the radiance of his love, peace, and joy (see 2 Cor 3:18).

Praying is like going to a service station to refuel so that I can continue my journey. Prayer refuels me for my mission in life.

8 *"Where two or three are gathered in my name, there am I in the midst of them."* (Mt 18:20)

My real dignity in life arises from the fact that I belong to the body of Christ. I am a member of the family of God. I belong to his community.

When I pray with others, Jesus is there praying with me and within me.

He healed the paralytic because of the faith of the community: Jesus, "saw their faith ..." (Lk 5:20).

Stay with me, Lord, and pray with me.

9 *[Jesus] took with him Peter and John and James, and went up on the mountain to pray.* (Lk 9:28)

Times for prayer and union with his Father had a very high priority for Jesus. Even though the crowds followed his every footstep, Jesus often escaped to spend time in prayer.

I often think that I am too busy to pray because there are so many demands made upon my time. I need to remind myself that I always find time to eat my meals. How much more essential is the spiritual food I need!

Jesus, take me up the mountain with you and teach me how to pray.

10 *We all, with unveiled face, beholding the glory of the Lord, are being changed into his likeness from one degree of glory to another; for this comes from the Lord who is the Spirit.* (2 Cor 3:18)

As I gaze on the Lord a powerful transforming effect is taking place within me—often without my even being aware of the process.

As I rest lovingly in the sunshine of his presence, he, like the sun, warms, nourishes, cheers, and transforms me. All he asks is my time.

"Come away by yourselves ... and rest a while" (Mk 6:31).

11 *Come to me; hear, that your soul may live.* (Is 55:3)

It is hard for me to realize that listening is praying. I listen when I just rest and relax in the Lord's presence. I listen as I permit God to love me, when I bask in the sunshine of his love. I need not say a single word; just being there and wanting him is enough.

Some may call it "wasting time," but with whom could I more profitably "waste time"?

12 *"Ask, and it will be given you; seek, and you will find; knock, and it will be opened to you."* (Mt 7:7)

God wants to be a gracious and generous Abba to me. However, he wants me to ask for whatever I need, not to make him aware of my needs, but to bring me to a deeper appreciation of my dependence on him.

Jesus instructs me simply and clearly how to pray with perseverance and patience. Furthermore, he gives me the assurance that I will receive and I will find.

All Jesus asks is faith and trust in him.

13 *"Rejoice in your hope, be patient in tribulation, be constant in prayer."* (Rom 12:12)

How frequently Scripture reminds me that I should pray always, pray without ceasing, persevere in prayer.

Quite obviously I cannot spend all my time in concentrated prayer, nor does God want that kind of prayer only. Prayer is my relationship with God. When I "rejoice in hope" I am praying, because it proves that my faith is sufficiently vibrant to trust and love God. When I accept God's will and am "patient under trial" I am also praying.

This kind of lifestyle means that I am persevering in prayer.

14 *In these days he went out to the mountain to pray; and all night he continued in prayer to God.* (Lk 6:12)

Jesus is teaching me a whole new dimension in prayer. His prayer was "in communion with God." Jesus was satisfied just to remain in a wordless communication with his Father.

He was teaching me that in prayer, I should be content just to remain in communion with God, my Father, to experience his presence, to bask in the sunshine of his love, to enjoy his peace. Then I will be enlightened to see his will and strengthened to fulfill it in my daily sojourn on earth.

"Abide in my love" (Jn 15:9).

15 *Pray constantly, give thanks in all circumstances.* (1 Thes 5:17)

An ungrateful person cannot be a prayerful person. If I were to pause to count the blessings God showers upon me every hour, it would set my mind whirling, for every heartbeat is a special gift from him.

If God's blessings are flowing profusely and constantly then my prayer of gratitude should be unceasing.

"O Lord, my God, I will give thanks to thee for ever" (Ps 30:12).

16 *"Truly, truly, I say to you, if you ask anything of the Father, he will give it to you in my name."* (Jn 16:23)

What does Jesus mean when he tells me to ask in his name? Surely he does not mean simply adding his name to my petition and my prayer.

Jesus wants me to have the same disposition, the same mentality, the same attitudes which were his when he came to prayer.

His attitude was total, loving, generous submission to the Father's will.

What greater example have I than his complete resignation to the Father's will at possibly the most crucial moment of his life on earth: "Father, if thou art willing, remove this cup from me; nevertheless not my will, but thine, be done" (Lk 22:42).

17 *"O my Lord, thou only art our King; help me, who am alone and have no helper but thee."* (Est 14:3b)

Esther's prayer is a perfect model for my prayer. Esther recognized the greatness and lordship of God. Her first concern was for his glory.

Her second concern was more comprehensive: she was praying for her people.

Esther realized her own poverty, her own human weakness. She prayed with great confidence and trust in the Lord.

Thank you, Lord, for showing me the way to prayer through your faithful servant Esther.

18 *He went up on the mountain by himself to pray.* (Mt 14:23)

Praying is like climbing a mountain. I must leave behind the preoccupations of each day. I must rise above the mundane and reach out in love to God, for "the heights of the mountains are his" (Ps 95:4).

As I climb the mountain my view becomes more cosmic, and therefore more Christlike. I can see beyond my own little world and pray more fervently for the coming of his kingdom to all my brothers and sisters throughout the world.

"Come, let us go up to the mountain of the Lord" (Is 2:3).

19 *I prayed, and understanding was given me.* (Wis 7:7)

I frequently find that decision making is difficult for me. I wonder just what God wants me to do in a given situation. His will often seems obscure.

Prayer is placing myself before the Lord as an empty vessel, prepared to receive whatever he wishes to give. When I do this in prayer, a solution to a perplexing problem often becomes crystal clear, even though I was not even thinking about the problem at the time.

"Teach me thy way, O Lord; and lead me on a level path" (Ps 27:11).

20 *"How much more will your Father who is in heaven give good things to those who ask him!"* (Mt 7:11)

Jesus encourages me to pray constantly and perseveringly for all my needs. He assures me once again of how much the Father loves me and wants everything that is good for me.

It gives the Father great joy when I acknowledge my dependence on him. The Father rejoices "to give good things to anyone who asks him."

"I give thee thanks, O Lord, with my whole heart" (Ps 138:1).

21 *As a hart longs for flowing streams, so longs my soul for thee, O God.* (Ps 42:1)

A longing for God, a hunger and thirst for his love, a desire to experience his presence is prayer of the highest order.

As a deer longs for running water, so my soul is restless until I find Jesus, my living water. He alone can bring me to the Father.

Prayer is the avenue which brings me into an experience of God. In solitude and silence I can come to know God in a way I have never before experienced.

22 *He withdrew to the wilderness and prayed.* (Lk 5:16)

The desert seems to be the ideal place for prayer. There I find the power and majesty of God in the expansive silence. There I discover that my survival depends on God's caring love.

At times I long for a desert experience. I can experience one when I enter the desert of solitude and silence in my own heart.

Jesus, lead me into the desert where I will find you waiting to meet me, and then fill me with your love.

23 *"Behold, I stand at the door and knock; if any one hears my voice and opens the door, I will come in to him and eat with him, and he with me."* (Rv 3:20)

My prayer posture must be one of quiet listening. Jesus reminds me that I will not hear him calling unless I listen with all my being.

When I listen I can welcome him into my heart and into my whole life. Listening will keep me experientially aware of his loving presence enveloping me.

Jesus, please keep knocking until I hear.

24 *"He who has ears to hear, let him hear."* (Mt 11:15)

God's mysteries are inscrutable. However, when I quietly listen to his Word I am blessed with new insights and deeper understanding.

When I listen, I am opening myself to the influence of the Holy Spirit who will endow me with his gifts of wisdom, knowledge, and understanding, as well as the gift of discernment.

"Come, Holy Spirit, and be my guest."

25 *"When you pray, go into your room and shut the door and pray to your Father who is in secret."* (Mt 6:6)

Jesus assures me that to form an intimate, personal relationship with the Father, I have to meet him privately and rest in his loving presence with a listening heart.

St. John of the Cross says: "The language that God hears best is the silent language of love."

It is in my silent listening that I, too, can best hear what God is saying to me.

Jesus, teach me the art of listening.

26 *"This is my beloved Son, with whom I am well pleased; listen to him."* (Mt 17:5)

How graciously the Father presents Jesus to us on Mount Tabor. The Father has only one request: "Listen to him."

Listening is loving because we are giving ourselves totally to another person. Listening is also praying.

Listening is an art. To listen I must put aside everything— my worries and anxieties, my hopes and ambitions, my programs and possibilities—to place myself in the warming rays of the sunshine of God's presence and give him my undivided attention.

This is one of the highest forms of prayer.

27 *Continue steadfastly in prayer, being watchful in it with thanksgiving.* (Col 4:2)

Prayer is being "attentive" to everything around me. God is present in all of his creation. He is present in me, sustaining and energizing me, giving me the ability to think and express my thoughts in words. He is inspiring and encouraging me, comforting and consoling me throughout the day. Above all, he is pouring out his love upon me at this very moment.

When I pause to recall his loving presence and power within me, then I am praying.

With Thomas I exclaim: "My Lord and my God!" (Jn 20:28).

28 *Mary kept all these things, pondering them in her heart.*
(Lk 2:19)

Like Mary's my life is filled with the mystery of God's love. I cannot fathom this love, nor can I respond to it unless I spend time in quiet, prayerful reflection.

Mary was a model disciple of Jesus. As she contemplated the mystery of God's salvific love and her role in its fulfillment, she could not but commit herself unreservedly to God's plan.

Mary, through your powerful intercession, obtain for me the grace of a prayerful and generous heart.

29 *"Ask, and you will receive, that your joy may be full."* (Jn 16:24)

Jesus wants me to be a happy, joyous disciple. He revealed the Good News of my redemption and the promise of eternal life to fill me with a joy which this world cannot give.

As he himself said: "These things I have spoken to you, that my joy may be in you, and that your joy may be full" (Jn 15:11).

Today, Jesus, I do come to "ask" and "receive" what you promised. In my prayer I ask that I may be filled with a deep, quiet, interior joy and become a channel of joy to everyone along the path I travel.

"Rejoice in the Lord always; again I will say, Rejoice" (Phil 4:4).

30 *"He who has ears, let him hear."* (Mt 13:43)

When Jesus urges me to heed what I hear, he is encouraging me to listen. I hear very much throughout the day, but I seldom listen.

It is not enough to hear God's Word; I must let it penetrate my whole being. Only in my prayer of listening will I begin to understand what Jesus is trying to say to me.

"Speak, for thy servant hears" (1 Sm 3:10).

31 *"Then you will call upon me and come and pray to me, and I will hear you. You will seek me and find me; when you seek me with all your heart."* (Jer 29:12-13)

Already through the prophets of the Old Testament God gives me the reassurance of his providential love. If I come to him faithfully and trustingly, he promises not only to grant my needs, but also to grant me a deeper, richer relationship with him as my loving Father.

I must seek him with all my heart by abandoning my own ambitions and personal interests. My attitude must be: Here I am, Lord, what is it you want of me today?

Part II
Conditioning

Conditioning

Learn from me; for I am gentle and lowly in heart.

MATTHEW 11:29

A recruit must be duly indoctrinated, educated, and trained before he can assume his responsibilities. Likewise, a disciple of Jesus must also be informed and transformed.

When a person recognizes his or her call from the Lord, a conversion or conditioning process must take place before he or she becomes a full-fledged disciple. Such a conditioning occurred even in the life of Joseph and Mary (see Mt 1:18-25).

Our brokenness prevents us from fully putting on the mind and the heart of Jesus. St. Paul encourages us in this conditioning process: "In your minds you must be the same as Christ Jesus" (Phil 2:5, JB). "Your mind must be renewed by a spiritual revolution ... put on the new self that has been created in God's way" (Eph 4:23-24, JB).

Nor is the process of conditioning ever complete. An ongoing conversion, a constant refocusing of our attention on Jesus, is imperative.

Jesus himself gave us a compendium of the attitudes and dispositions necessary for a disciple and set forth these conditions in the Beatitudes.

In the first three Beatitudes Jesus points out the obstacles to that spiritual perfection expected of his disciples: love of

51

wealth; pride of race, learning, or power; and the inordinate desire for pleasure.

In the second three Beatitudes Jesus outlines right conduct toward God, our neighbor, and ourselves: justice, mercy, single-heartedness.

In the last two Beatitudes Jesus invites his disciples to labor in spreading the gospel of peace and to expect as a reward persecution and suffering.

In effect Jesus said that he was poor in spirit, sorrowful, lowly, holy, merciful, single-hearted, a peacemaker, and a victim of persecution; and blessed will we be if we are like him. Each Beatitude is a formation process for the devoted disciple.

As we listen at the core of our being to what Jesus is telling us in each Beatitude in the next eight chapters, we will experience the power of his Word to mold, shape, and form us into determined, dedicated disciples.

His Word will also be the source of our encouragement and strength, our power and perseverance. We will follow him to be all that he wants us to be.

Prayer

Take, Lord, and receive all my liberty,
my memory, my understanding, and my entire will—
all that I have and call my own.
You have given it all to me.
To you, Lord, I return it.
Everything is yours; do with it what you will.
Give me only your love and your grace.
That is enough for me.

St. Ignatius of Loyola

To Be Poor in Spirit

Blessed are the poor in spirit, for theirs is the kingdom of heaven.
MATTHEW 5:3

Poverty of spirit means many things. It first of all means a detachment from material possessions which might rule our lives.

Jesus set the pace for us. Consider the starkness of Bethlehem, the foreignness of Egypt, the barrenness of Nazareth.

In his public life he had nowhere to lay his head (see Mt 8:20). In his dying moments, after he gave us his Mother, he saw the soldiers gambling for his last earthly possession—his seamless tunic.

Poverty of spirit also means a recognition of our own inadequacy and our own inability to accomplish anything of ourselves.

Again Jesus showed us the way. He always turned to his Father to ascertain his will, to seek his help, and to thank him for his love.

If we want to be his disciples, we must be poor in spirit. This is the first step in the process of conditioning. May the following scriptural texts guide us in becoming poor in spirit.

1 *"Blessed are the poor in spirit, for theirs is the kingdom of heaven."*
(Mt 5:3)

Jesus is saying to me: "I am poor in spirit, and blest will you be if you follow me in becoming poor in spirit."

Poverty of spirit means true humility which helps me to recognize that of myself I am nothing, but with Jesus I can do all things. It is the truth about myself and the truth about God.

Poverty of spirit is my first step in becoming a true disciple.

2 *Jesus said to him, "Foxes have holes, and birds of the air have nests; but the Son of man has nowhere to lay his head."* (Mt 8:20)

How graphically, yet how emphatically, Jesus sets himself forth as the model of detachment!

Jesus, I know that when my will is attached to earthly things my heart is not free. Let me experience the joy of clinging to your will alone, so that my heart will be free to listen to your Word and to love you.

3 *Have this mind among yourselves, which is yours in Christ Jesus who ... emptied himself, taking the form of a servant ... obedient unto death, even death on a cross.* (Phil 2:5-8)

Jesus is the transcendent God of heaven and earth, yet he took the form of a slave because he loves with an infinite love.

Love must give and the greater the love, the greater the giving.

Listen to Jesus ask: "Do you love me?" (Jn 21:16).

4 *"You lack one thing; go, sell what you have, and give to the poor, and you will have treasure in heaven; and come, follow me."*

(Mk 10:21)

Like this man, I tenaciously hold on to what I think I have earned, merited, or worked for in life.

How difficult for me to realize that everything is his gift, and these material possessions are loaned to me by God to be used for his greater honor and glory!

"Each one must do as he has made up his mind, not reluctantly or under compulsion, for God loves a cheerful giver" (2 Cor 9:7).

5 *For you know the grace of our Lord Jesus Christ, that though he was rich, yet for your sake he became poor, so that by his poverty you might become rich.* (2 Cor 8:9)

Jesus loves me so much that he was willing to suffer, die, and rise again from the dead so that he could share his divine life with me, making me the temple of the Holy Spirit.

This greatest treasure calls forth unbounded gratitude.

6 *Mary said, "My soul magnifies the Lord, and my spirit rejoices in God my Savior."* (Lk 1:46)

In all humility Mary sings of the greatness of the Lord because God who is mighty has done great things for her (see Lk 1:49).

When I acknowledge that all that I am and all that I have has come from God, then my heart, too, will sing the joy of the Lord.

"Great is our Lord, and abundant in power; his understanding is beyond measure" (Ps 147:5).

7 *The prayer of a poor man goes from his lips to the ears of God, and his judgment comes speedily.* (Sir 21:5)

God wants to be a generous and loving Abba, but I must be disposed to receive his beneficence.

Poverty of spirit helps me to recognize my total and complete dependence on God. When I come in weakness, then God fills me with his strength.

With St. Paul I say: "I thank him who has given me strength for this, Christ Jesus our Lord, because he judged me faithful by appointing me to his service" (1 Tm 1:12).

8 *"They need not go away; you give them something to eat." ... "We have only five loaves here and two fish."* (Mt 14:16-17)

It was only after the apostles realized that they were unable to feed the large crowd which came to listen to Jesus, that Jesus stepped in. Only after they admitted their own poverty and manifested their total dependence on him did Jesus multiply the loaves and fishes.

Jesus deals with me in the same way. When I am weak, he strengthens me; when I am needy, he fills me—but only after I acknowledge my own poverty.

"Give us this day our daily bread" (Mt 6:11).

9 *"He must increase, but I must decrease."* (Jn 3:30)

These words of John the Baptist corroborate Jesus' estimation that no man is greater than John.

Am I hurt or disappointed if someone is chosen in preference to me? Or am I happy and delighted when someone else is honored?

Do I permit Jesus to increase in me by letting my own ideas, ambitions, and self-will decrease?

10 *What have you that you did not receive? If then you received it, why do you boast as if it were not a gift?* (1 Cor 4:7)

How apt I am to boast of my own gifts and accomplishments as if I were personally responsible for them! How often I need to recall Jesus' words: "Apart from me you can do nothing" (Jn 15:5).

Thank you, Lord, for gifting me. May I use all your gifts for your honor and glory.

11 *"He who is greatest among you shall be your servant."* (Mt 23:11)

How direct is Jesus' instruction and admonition! If I am to be a genuine follower of Jesus, I must reach out in loving service to everyone without distinction.

"As you did it to one of the least of these my brethren, you did it to me" (Mt 25:40). How rewarding!

12 *Indeed I count everything as loss because of the surpassing worth of knowing Christ Jesus my Lord. For his sake I have suffered the loss of all things, and count them as refuse, in order that I may gain Christ.* (Phil 3:8)

Many things were important to me when I was a child, but as I grew older, these things lost their appeal. In fact, I disdained them as toys of a time long ago.

As I form a deeper and more personal relationship with Jesus, the enticements and allurements of this world lose much of their glitter. Some even appear as rubbish now.

Thank you, Jesus, for this change of heart.

13 *He said to me, "My grace is sufficient for you, for my power is made perfect in weakness." I will all the more gladly boast of my weaknesses, that the power of Christ may rest upon me.* (2 Cor 12:9)

I need Jesus at every moment of the day. When I am aware of my own weakness and my complete dependence upon him, then I am growing in holiness. It is then that Jesus will empower me, making me strong with his strength, confident with his support.

When Jesus said, "Apart from me you can do nothing," he was really saying that with him I can do all things.

14 *As each has received a gift, employ it for one another, as good stewards of God's varied grace.* (1 Pt 4:10)

Realizing that the gifts and talents which I have are really special gifts loaned to me from God makes me more grateful. Then I more readily recognize that I must use them graciously and generously for others.

By using these gifts prudently, I express my gratitude to God for entrusting me with them.

15 *Now the company of those who believed were of one heart and soul, and no one said that any of the things which he possessed was his own, but they had everything in common.* (Acts 4:32)

The early Christians, who lived in community, manifested their love for one another and their poverty of spirit by their mutual dependence on each other.

I, too, can live my poverty of spirit by my dependence on others as I live and work with my brothers and sisters in Christ. My confidence and trust in others manifests my love for them.

Just as the early Christians gave witness to their world, I can give witness in the little world that I call home.

16 *On the day I called, thou didst answer me, my strength of soul thou didst increase.* (Ps 138:3)

When I find myself unable to cope with a certain situation and turn to the Lord in humble prayer, I am being poor in spirit. This prayer posture is always pleasing to my loving Father. His heart is ever overflowing, and he wants to respond graciously and generously to all my needs.

Thank you for being such a provident Father.

17 *"The Son of man also came not to be served but to serve, and to give his life as a ransom for many."* (Mk 10:45)

Jesus, you were not satisfied with just telling me how to live a life of service for others—but you paved the way for me by your own example. Continue to remind me that my life of service to others is the only real gateway to happiness in this life and a certain path to you.

Today, as a special act of loving service, let me touch the most "undesirable" brother or sister.

18 *"Lay up for yourselves treasures in heaven, where neither moth nor rust consumes and where thieves do not break in and steal."* (Mt 6:20)

I can become unduly concerned about the ephemeral aspects of my life—reputation, recognition, pleasure, possessions, status symbols. The more I keep my focus on the Lord and my final destiny, the better I am able to realize how fleeting and empty are these standards of the world. They cannot satisfy the void in my heart.

Thank you, Jesus, for your words of wisdom.

19 *"Therefore do not be anxious about tomorrow, for tomorrow will be anxious for itself. Let the day's own trouble be sufficient for the day."* (Mt 6:34)

Worry and anxiety are negative extremes which are often employed by the evil one. On the other hand, care and concern are born of faith and trust in God.

When I keep my will in tune with God's will, I can step out confidently each day knowing that nothing will happen which God does not will or permit for my own good.

"Today is the tomorrow that I was worrying about yesterday, but it did not happen."

20 *He who mocks the poor insults his Maker; he who is glad at calamity will not go unpunished.* (Prv 17:5)

In Jesus' day a person's poverty was looked upon as a sign of God's disfavor on that person, whereas material blessings were considered a proof of their goodness and holiness. Jesus tried to dispel this false notion by his teachings and his own example.

I must be on my guard not to fall into this same trap—equating poverty with shiftlessness, indolence, and ignorance.

Father, help me to recognize my own poverty and my total dependence on you.

21 *He only is my rock and my salvation.* (Ps 62:2)

How apt I am to seek the pot of gold at the end of every rainbow! How often I have been disillusioned in pursuing so many mundane ambitions!

After these experiences I can realize the veracity of St. Augustine's famous expression: "Our hearts are restless until they rest in you, Lord."

Lord, help me to adopt and abide by this maxim.

22 *In those days Jesus came from Nazareth of Galilee and was baptized by John in the Jordan.* (Mk 1:9)

What poverty Jesus manifested in his life. He humbly submitted to this rite of repentance even though he was sinless, even though he came to conquer sin. Jesus came to serve. He emptied himself.

Jesus did all this for me because he was trying to teach me by his example his way of life. When I acknowledge my poverty of spirit, then Jesus can fill me with his strength and power, with his love and with that joy which the world cannot give.

23 *He went down with them and came to Nazareth, and was obedient to them.* (Lk 2:51)

Jesus, the Lord of heaven and earth, was obedient to his creatures. What condescension! What humility!

In order to mature in my spiritual growth, I must be receptive to the guidance and direction of those God sends into my life. I must be humble enough to open my heart and soul to a prayer companion. Some aspects of my way of life might be challenged. I might have to change some of my pet habits.

Jesus, you challenge me by your own example, for you were "obedient to them."

24 *"Is not this the carpenter, the son of Mary?"* (Mk 6:3)

Jesus could not be considered a teacher in his culture because he had to work for a living and was poor.

Jesus added so much dignity to work. My ability to work is a share in God's creative plan. God brought the world to a certain stage of perfection. He wants me to help bring it to a higher state of perfection through my own work.

My work is also a way of reaching out in love to others. Jesus showed me the way by his own example.

25 *O how abundant is thy goodness, which thou hast laid up for those who fear thee, and wrought for those who take refuge in thee, in the sight of the sons of men!* (Ps 31:19)

God will never abandon me when I come to him in trust and in a spirit of poverty. He will pour out upon me his providential love along with peace and protection. His goodness will not only be manifested in a private or invisible way, but also publicly—"in the sight of men."

He asks only my proper dispositions: a recognition of my need for his protective love and an implicit trust in him.

26 *For he was crucified in weakness, but lives by the power of God. For we are weak in him, but in dealing with you we shall live with him by the power of God.* (2 Cor 13:4)

What poverty of spirit Jesus manifested by submitting to the torturous death on the cross! He, whose almighty power created and controls the universe, was gentle as a lamb. His weakness was so powerful it redeemed a sinful world.

Being genuinely poor in spirit enables me to accept the fruits of his redeeming love. Endowed with his presence and power within me, I will be able to follow him as a true disciple.

27 *"Truly, I say to you, whoever does not receive the kingdom of God like a child shall not enter it."* (Lk 18:17)

How trusting a little child can be! How great is its simple, trusting faith! The child asks for no proofs, no guarantees; he is confident that others will be true to their word.

A child's attitude is one of complete confidence and trust.

Jesus holds up a little child as a model for me. He encourages me to let a little child show me the way into the kingdom of God.

28 *Love bears all things, believes all things, hopes all things, endures all things.* (1 Cor 13:7)

In his classic dissertation on love, St. Paul summarizes my response to love in just a few words. If I truly love another person, I will really trust him or her. I can depend on that person in my own hour of need or weakness.

Great as another person's love for me may be, it is infinitesimal compared with the love which Jesus has for me. How much greater should my trust be in him!

"I believe; help my unbelief!" (Mk 9:24).

29 *"Do not fear, only believe."* (Mk 5:36)

Fear can be debilitating, even paralyzing. If it is out of control it causes worry and anxiety. It can rob me of the peace and happiness which the Lord wants me to enjoy.

In the spiritual realm, the effects of fear can be disastrous. Jesus puts it briefly, but adequately: "Fear is useless."

Jesus tells me that what I need is trust and confidence in him if I am to grow and mature in my relationship with him.

30 *"Let not your hearts be troubled; believe in God, believe also in me."* (Jn 14:1)

Jesus spoke these words to me the night before he died. The fact that they are his "last will and testament" to me adds greater urgency to his request.

Jesus fulfilled every promise he ever made. Why should I not trust him now?

Jesus is the Way, and the Truth, and the Life; I can go to the Father only through him.

Lord, here are all my worries and anxieties; I give them all to you, so that I can trust you completely.

31 *As for the rich in this world, charge them not to be haughty, nor to set their hopes on uncertain riches but on God who richly furnishes us with everything to enjoy.* (1 Tm 6:17)

My provident Father, who cares for the birds of the air and the wildflowers in the field, loves me with an overwhelming love. His love cannot change. It cannot be any greater; it is infinite.

I cannot merit, deserve, or gain his love. He freely gives it. In fact, my Father rejoices in pouring out his love on me by providing whatever I need.

All he asks is that I depend on him and trust him. When I place my implicit trust in his loving care and concern for me, I am expressing my own loving response and also my gratitude.

That is the mystery which love holds.

To Be Sorrowing

Blessed are those who mourn, for they shall be comforted.

MATTHEW 5:4

In his human nature Jesus suffered every pain, sorrow, and hurt which we must endure from time to time.

Jesus was a "man of sorrows." He wept over the unbelief of Jerusalem and experienced the humiliating pain of rejection. He was deserted by his disciples—denied by Peter, betrayed by Judas.

Jesus' greatest sorrow was the realization that his people were rejecting their own redemption and eternal happiness.

When sorrow rends our hearts we will find great consolation from the moment we are able to accept suffering as part of God's plan for us.

Jesus says to us:

I experienced the depth of sorrow, but found consolation in doing my Father's will. Blest too will you be when sorrow comes your way, for I will be your consolation.

1 *"Blessed are those who mourn, for they shall be comforted."* (Mt 5:4)

Sorrow springs from love. When I am sorry about my many faults and failures, when I am sorry about the sinfulness of the world, then I am loving the Lord.

When I am sympathetic to others and empathetic with the poor, the suffering, the downtrodden—then I am reaching out in love to my neighbor.

This sorrowing will be specially blessed by God because I am loving as Jesus wants me to love.

2 *"Truly, truly, I say to you, you will weep and lament, but the world will rejoice; you will be sorrowful, but your sorrow will turn into joy."* (Jn 16:20)

Jesus does not trick anyone into following him or becoming his disciple. He tells it as it is.

While he prepares me for the hardships and sufferings of life, he also assures me that these are transitory, and in the end I will have that joy which the world cannot give.

Jesus, I will be happy to take all the joys you want to give me—as soon as you want to give them!

3 *"If any man would come after me, let him deny himself and take up his cross and follow me."* (Mt 16:24)

Each time I die to myself—to my own self-interests and selfish whims—I open myself to the outpouring of God's divine life. As he takes over more and more in my life, I will begin to walk in his footsteps.

Jesus, give me time; don't walk too fast.

4 *He heals the brokenhearted and binds up their wounds.* (Ps 147:3)

Jesus does not ask me to suffer anything which he has not already endured. He experienced the pain of a broken heart. How eager he is to assure me of his abiding presence and love when I am faced with great pain or sorrow!

He is the "God of all comfort" (2 Cor 1:3).

5 *In those days Jesus came from Nazareth of Galilee and was baptized by John in the Jordan.* (Mk 1:9)

This is only a brief statement, but I can read the pain between the lines. Jesus left the hallowed confines of his home in Nazareth to begin his public ministry.

What sorrow must have filled his heart as he left his Mother and the protective peace and security of his own village! What blessings his leaving home brought to an unredeemed world!

I am likewise called, but how reluctant I am to accept the pain of separation. Jesus, give me strength and generosity to follow your example.

6 *"Blessed are you when men revile you and persecute you and utter all kinds of evil against you falsely on my account. Rejoice and be glad, for your reward is great in heaven, for so men persecuted the prophets who were before you."* (Mt 5:11-12)

At first these words of Jesus seem incongruous. Pain, persecution, and rejection normally wound me deeply and rob me of peace.

However, when I see suffering as a splinter of the cross of Jesus, I can think of myself as another Simon of Cyrene. When I unite my pain with the suffering of Jesus, I can truly "rejoice and be glad."

7 *If you turn to him with all your heart and with all your soul, to do what is true before him, then he will turn to you and will not hide his face from you.* (Tb 13:6)

The sorrow which Jesus pronounced blessed is not a whining self-pity, but rather that sorrow which impels me to turn back to him with all my heart.

This beatitude then becomes identified with the precept to rejoice in the Lord always (see Phil 4:4).

As his disciple I must sometimes smile through my tears, letting his joy permeate all my sorrows.

Lord, may your face shine forth from me always.

8 *Rejoice in so far as you share Christ's sufferings, that you may also rejoice and be glad when his glory is revealed.* (1 Pt 4:13)

There is a mystery and a power about suffering. I try to avoid it, yet I have discovered that it is a means of keeping in close union with the Lord.

In suffering I recognize my need of my heavenly Father's healing love. Suffering detaches me from the frivolous and mundane in my life and keeps me in touch with Jesus.

How rightly Jesus said: "Blest too are the sorrowing."

9 *"O Jerusalem, Jerusalem, killing the prophets and stoning those who are sent to you! How often would I have gathered your children together as a hen gathers her brood under her wings, and you would not!"* (Lk 13:34)

I want to be accepted and loved so much that a fear of rejection lingers with me always. Jesus, too, wants me to accept him so that through my acceptance I will be happy with him in heaven for all eternity. Listen to his plaintive lament: "and you refused me."

I am sorry, Jesus! May I accept you and your divine will in everything this day.

10 *For I do not do the good I want, but the evil I do not want is what I do.* (Rom 7:19)

How right you are, St. Paul! You have taken the words right out of my mouth!

However, Jesus, I know you look at my fundamental desire.

Yes, I do want to serve you. I do want to do what you ask of me. Since I earnestly desire to do your will, forgive my excursions to the right or to the left. Bring me back on target.

11 *Rejoice with those who rejoice, weep with those who weep.* (Rom 12:15)

If I love a person I want to share the joys and sorrows of life with that person. By sharing his or her sorrow I will lighten the burden of the pain. By sharing the joy I will double the happiness it brings.

Thank you, Paul, for reminding me.

12 *It is not an enemy who taunts me, then I could bear it.... But it is you, my equal, my companion, my familiar friend.* (Ps 55:12-13)

Jesus suffered the treachery of Judas, the denial of Peter, the desertion of all the other disciples. He accepted this suffering in order to caution me not to abandon him, and also to prepare me for the times when similar experiences would come my way.

Surely he is a God of consolation!

13 *"O my people, what have I done to you? In what have I wearied you? Answer me!"* (Mi 6:3)

These words which I hear every Holy Week remind me that Jesus endured every pain which I am asked to bear. His plaintive question touches my heart, for I, too, have caused him some of this pain.

Jesus, let me answer you by saying that I am sorry and thanking you for your forgiveness.

14 *Look and see if there is any sorrow like my sorrow.* (Lam 1:12)

When I am tempted to wallow in self-pity or be hemmed in by the circle of my self-centeredness I can always recall these words spoken of Jesus' suffering. As I listen I can hear Jesus ask if I am willing to accept a few of the splinters of his cross.

How could I refuse such a little burden?

15 *When he drew near and saw the city he wept over it, saying, "Would that even today you knew the things that make for peace! But now they are hid from your eyes."* (Lk 19:41-42)

Let me just sit with Jesus on the slope of Mount Olivet and be with him as he weeps. Words fail me. I do not have to say anything, just strive to experience what Jesus must have felt.

Jesus, never let me lose sight of you in my daily ramblings.

16 *Restore to me the joy of thy salvation, and uphold me with a willing spirit.* (Ps 51:12)

Sorrow is always accompanied by a willingness to change, to rectify, to make amends. A change of heart is not possible without the help of God and his special grace.

Lord, give me a new heart and a new spirit. Enable me to persevere in my resolve to love more intently.

17 *"Father, I have sinned against heaven and before you; I am no longer worthy to be called your son."* (Lk 15:18-19)

I could make these words of the Prodigal Son my own, for I, too, have sinned. The contrite attitude of the younger son stole the father's heart. Likewise, my repentant heart brings joy to Jesus who wants to continue his redemptive, forgiving, healing, purifying, sanctifying work within me. All he asks is my humble admission and contrition.

18 *Looking to Jesus the pioneer and perfecter of our faith, who for the joy that was set before him endured the cross, despising the shame.* (Heb 12:2)

When I keep my eyes fixed on Jesus, everything else in life becomes peripheral. When trials, difficulties, misunderstandings, hardships seem to block my way, all I need to do is keep Jesus in focus as he trudges along the dreadful way of the cross. Suddenly my cross becomes a featherweight.

19 *Going a little farther he fell on his face and prayed, "My Father, if it be possible, let this cup pass from me; nevertheless, not as I will, but as thou wilt."* (Mt 26:39)

What an insuperable burden Jesus was asked to accept in the Garden of Gethsemane. In that dreadful hour he faced one of the greatest human decisions ever made. Only after praying intensely was he able to say yes to the Father.

Jesus, in the little decisions which I face today, let me say with you: "Not as I will, but as thou wilt."

20 *He will not let you be tempted beyond your strength, but with the temptation will also provide the way of escape, that you may be able to endure it.* (1 Cor 10:13)

Sometimes a cross seems too painful and heavy a burden. I may even get angry about my lot in life. I must remember that testings strengthen and mature me, and make me more Christlike.

Jesus is always with me, carrying the greater share of the burden.

21 *As we share abundantly in Christ's sufferings, so through Christ we share abundantly in comfort too.* (2 Cor 1:5)

Each time the Lord permits some little pain or hardship to come my way, he is asking me to help him carry a slight portion of his cross. Paul reminds me that every trial in life is a steppingstone into my union with God. What a consolation!

Lord, if I could only remember this each time a little cross surprises me and trips me up as I am striving to walk in your footprints!

22 *"My God, my God, why hast thou forsaken me?"* (Mt 27:46)

In praying this psalm (Ps 22:2), Jesus wanted me to know how much he felt abandoned ... apparently even by his Father. Jesus is reassuring me that he will always be with me, and that I never face any pain or sorrow alone.

"I am with you always; yes, to the end of time." (Mt 28:20, JB).

23 *"Behold the man!"* (Jn 19:5)

This pathetic scene—Jesus appearing on Pilate's judgment seat before the crowd, scourged, crowned with thorns, mocked as a king—moves me into a deeper spirit of compassion. Jesus willingly accepted this terrible physical pain and horrible humiliation because he loves me.

May this picture of Jesus, so maltreated, be indelibly impressed on my heart that I may willingly, even if reluctantly, accept whatever suffering comes my way, and unite it to the passion of Jesus.

Then I will be truly blessed.

24 *If we confess our sins, he is faithful and just, and will forgive our sins and cleanse us from all unrighteousness.* (1 Jn 1:9)

The Lord does not look so much at what I do, but rather at the disposition of my heart. Am I willing to acknowledge my sinfulness? Do I recognize my need for his redeeming love? If so, I know that I am forgiven and cleansed of every sin.

"To sin is human; to forgive is divine." Thank you, Jesus!

25 *Then they left the presence of the council, rejoicing that they were counted worthy to suffer dishonor for the name.* (Acts 5:41)

After having witnessed the sufferings, death, and resurrection of Jesus, the apostles understood a little better the reason for persecution. They united their ill-treatment with the rejection and suffering of Jesus for the sake of the kingdom. This gave a new meaning and a new dimension to the mystery of their own suffering.

Jesus, let this thought and attitude dominate my reaction to whatever crosses come into my life.

26 *"Truly, truly, I say to you, you will weep and lament, but the world will rejoice; you will be sorrowful, but your sorrow will turn into joy."* (Jn 16:20)

Grief is a cleansing, purifying, healing balm. By sweeping away the encumbrances which impede my progress into a close union with Jesus, it helps me concentrate on the real purpose of life. It keeps me on the straight and narrow, and helps me avoid the tangents which might lead me astray.

Jesus, let me unite my suffering to yours and find that joy you promised.

27 *Bear one another's burdens, and so fulfil the law of Christ.* (Gal 6:2)

When I go to another in need, I fulfill the law of love which Jesus laid down. I can help others carry their burdens not simply by trying to cheer them up or by urging them to smile and be happy. A more powerful means is to encourage them to unite their trials and sorrows to the suffering of Jesus. Compassion means to suffer *with*.

Jesus encourages me to come to him when I am heavily burdened and promises to refresh me (see Mt 11:28).

28

"I have not come to call the righteous, but sinners to repentance." (Lk 5:32)

Lord, how self-righteous I am! How often I sit in judgment on others! How slow I am to remember that "but for the grace of God, there go I."

Jesus, even though I am so self-righteous, don't abandon me, but keep inviting me to a change of heart. And grant me the grace to respond to your invitation.

29

[God] comforts us in all our affliction, so that we may be able to comfort those who are in any affliction, with the comfort with which we ourselves are comforted by God. (2 Cor 1:4)

If I have experienced the loving care and concern that Jesus has for me when I am lonely, discouraged, misunderstood, angry, sick, or in pain, I will be more able to comfort "those in trouble."

To experience Jesus' love for me is the greatest consolation I could have on this earth. How eager I should be to share this consolation with others.

Jesus, may I lead others to a deep, personal "heart" knowledge of you as a person. Then they, too, will know your consolation.

30 *"Those whom I love, I reprove and chasten; so be zealous and repent."* (Rv 3:19)

When I love a person I want that person to be as perfect as possible so that everyone can see his or her goodness. When I come close to Jesus, he makes me aware of my self-centeredness, my lack of sensitivity to others, my faults and failings.

He does so because he loves me and wants me to be able to radiate his image to others.

Thank you, Jesus, for reproving me and not giving up on me.

31 *For this slight momentary affliction is preparing for us an eternal weight of glory beyond all comparison.* (2 Cor 4:17)

Suffering holds its own locked-in secret. I will never be able to penetrate its mystery.

However, Jesus reassures me that the royal way of the cross is the surest path to eternal bliss. Each moment of suffering brings me into a closer union with him, and that union is what heaven is all about.

That is why St. Paul could say: "I consider that the sufferings of this present time are not worth comparing with the glory that is to be revealed to us" (Rom 8:18). And St. Peter adds: "This is a cause of great joy" (1 Pt 1:6, JB).

To Be Lowly

Blessed are the meek, for they shall inherit the earth.

MATTHEW 5:5

The life of a would-be follower of Jesus is beset with many paradoxes and dilemmas. The world strongly beckons a hopeful disciple to a way of life which is diametrically opposed to the standards which Jesus set. The world encourages us to dominate, conquer, succeed at any price, while Jesus says, "Blessed are the meek."

These two opposing standards are envisioned by Matthew in his account of the two banquets (see Mt 14:1-21). The banquet of Herod ended in debauchery and murder, while the guests at the banquet of Jesus were totally filled by his Word and the food miraculously provided. "All ate and were satisfied."

The following scriptural passages are suggested for each day of the coming month. These words of the Lord will help us walk the path which Jesus mapped out for the meek to inherit their heavenly homeland.

1 *"Blessed are the meek, for they shall inherit the earth."* (Mt 5:5)

Jesus, you were despised by so many: if I am to be your disciple I should not seek honors. Jesus, you were poor; money should not be my primary preoccupation. Jesus, you earned a living by hard work; I should not live idly. Jesus, you traveled on foot; I should not be concerned about a status-symbol type of transportation.

Jesus, teach me to live in a spirit of detachment.

2 *"Truly, I say to you, unless you turn and become like children, you will never enter the kingdom of heaven."* (Mt 18:3)

Everyone loves the simplicity and humility, the innocence and openness, the trust and confidence of a little child. Our hearts naturally reach out to such a child.

What a choice paragon Jesus selected for my imitation and emulation!

Jesus, let me step out today with the loving trust and confidence of a child. May your heart reach out in love to me.

3 *Humble yourselves therefore under the mighty hand of God, that in due time he may exalt you.* (1 Pt 5:6)

I am humble when I am able to say yes to all the laws of God. When I recognize that God is my loving Father, deeply concerned about me, then I recognize his laws as norms and directives to help me reach happiness in this life. This is the first degree of humility.

Jesus, you showed me the way. Teach me to follow your example.

4 *"Take my yoke upon you, and learn from me; for I am gentle and lowly in heart, and you will find rest for your souls. For my yoke is easy, and my burden is light."* (Mt 11:29-30)

Jesus, you are inviting me into the second degree of humility. My awareness of your enduring love for me helps me know that everything which happens in my daily routine is for your honor and glory and my own good.

Your yoke is easy when I realize it is *your* yoke and you are only asking me to help you carry it. You are gentle and humble. Come what may, I rejoice in your kindness to me.

5 *He was oppressed, and he was afflicted, yet he opened not his mouth; like a lamb that is led to the slaughter, and like a sheep that before its shearers is dumb, so he opened not his mouth.* (Is 53:7)

In this prophecy, Jesus led the way for me into the third degree of humility. If I am really humble, then I will prefer to be more like Jesus. He was insulted; therefore, I will prefer insults to honors, poverty to riches, humiliation to praise.

What a big order! But with Jesus leading the way and breaking ground for me, there is hope I may at least partially succeed.

6 *"Foxes have holes, and birds of the air have nests; but the Son of man has nowhere to lay his head."* (Mt 8:20)

Jesus, you were simply clothed, ill-nourished, poorly housed. If I am to be your witness, radiating your presence in my own surroundings, then I cannot be overly concerned about being fashionably clothed, sumptuously nourished, and richly housed.

Jesus, you wanted to be lowly; why should I have lofty ambitions and aspirations of greatness?

Jesus, endow me with the gifts and graces to follow the way you mapped out.

7 *"For every one who exalts himself will be humbled, and he who humbles himself will be exalted."* (Lk 14:11)

My insecurity prompts me to exalt myself. I fear nonacceptance, even rejection; hence I boast about my gifts and talents, my feats and accomplishments as though I were personally responsible for them.

On the contrary, when I admit that I am inadequate without the Lord's help, he will see that I am exalted in his sight.

8 *Rejoice greatly ... Shout aloud ... Lo, your king comes to you;... humble and riding on an ass, on a colt the foal of an ass.*
(Zec 9:9)

In biblical times the donkey was a symbol of peace, while the horse stood for war. Jesus came to reestablish our peace with the Father. In all humility he accepted our human nature with all its limitations.

His entry into Jerusalem was a great triumph because he came in all humility riding upon a donkey.

As I contemplate his utter humility, prompted by his love for me, I can rejoice heartily, and I do shout with joy.

9 *He went down with them and came to Nazareth.* (Lk 2:51)

There is great mystery shrouded in the solitude of that little home in Nazareth. Nazareth speaks to me of poverty, lowliness, littleness.

Nazareth radiates silence, solitude, humility, gentleness, prayerfulness.

Some looked upon Nazareth with indifference and contempt ... "Can anything good come from Nazareth?" (Jn 1:46).

Jesus, create a Nazareth in my heart.

10 *"Those who are well have no need of a physician, but those who are sick; I came not to call the righteous, but sinners."*

(Mk 2:17)

Jesus, you were always found among the sick, the suffering, and all those who were considered the outcasts of the society of your day. You were the friend of those who had no friends.

Jesus, you were the poorest among the poor, but you brought them the riches of your friendship and love.

Let me become your friend so that I can become a friend to all those who come my way.

11 *Let no one seek his own good, but the good of his neighbor.* (1 Cor 10:24)

What a paradox I face each day! By nature I am selfish and self-centered. I instinctively think that the more I get, the happier I will be. Yet I have so often experienced the contrary. When I give of myself, I find greater joy and happiness.

How true the adage: It is more blessed to give than to receive.

12 *Be subject to one another out of reverence for Christ.* (Eph 5:21)

How unequivocally and how clearly Jesus set forth the truth of his indwelling in every one of us! "Truly, I say to you, as you did it to one of the least of these my brethren, you did it to me" (Mt 25:40).

How slow I am to recognize Jesus in the people I deal with each day.

13 *Mary said: "Behold, I am the handmaid of the Lord; let it be to me according to your word."* (Lk 1:38)

After one brief clarification, Mary acquiesced wholeheartedly to the request of the angelic visitor, even though, humanly speaking, the request seemed preposterous.

That acquiescence helped redeem a world. Mary is my model for saying yes to the impossible.

Jesus reminds me: "All things are possible to him who believes" (Mk 9:23).

14 *Every good endowment and every perfect gift is from above, coming down from the Father of lights with whom there is no variation or shadow due to change.* (Jas 1:17)

True humility is knowing and acting on the truth about myself and the truth about God. I am humble when I acknowledge my dependence upon God. That pleases him.

Everything I have and am is gift. This truth makes my heart overflow with gratitude.

When I realize that all is gift, I want to show my gratitude by using every gift well. Thank you, Lord, for *everything*.

15 *Being found in human form he humbled himself and became obedient unto death, even death on a cross.* (Phil 2:8)

Death by crucifixion was the most painful and the most shameful kind of execution known in Jesus' day. Jesus humbled himself obediently to give me the example and motivation I need to take up my little cross each day.

My daily cross is made up of the little pinpricks—the disappointments and misunderstandings, the tensions and anxieties, the frustrations and failures which are part of my daily lot in life.

Thank you, Jesus, for encouraging me by setting the pace for me.

16 *"If I then, your Lord and Teacher, have washed your feet, you also ought to wash one another's feet."* (Jn 13:14)

Jesus washed the feet of his disciples not only as a gesture of humility, but even more: it was a manifestation of love. Washing their feet symbolized that they belonged to him, to his kingdom.

My service to others must always respect their dignity as persons. I must make them aware that they have a place in my heart.

17 *"If any one forces you to go one mile, go with him two miles."* (Mt 5:41)

If I try to help those in need, I can expect some people to take advantage of me. Stay, Jesus says: go that extra mile.

Someone expressed it so well: "If I help someone who deserves it, that is justice. I help someone who does not deserve it, that is charity."

Scripture says: "Do all for the glory of God" (1 Cor 10:31).

18 *"For the Son of man also came not to be served but to serve, and to give his life as a ransom for many."* (Mk 10:45)

When I contemplate the fact that Jesus gave his whole life for my salvation—from his first breath in Bethlehem to his last gasp on the cross—can I be niggardly in giving myself to the Father's will?

Jesus' life of service was a life of giving love.

Jesus came that I may have life and have it to the full (see Jn 10:10). I must be receptive to such extravagant generosity.

19 *At that time Jesus declared, "I thank thee, Father, Lord of heaven and earth, that thou hast hidden these things from the wise and understanding and revealed them to babes."* (Mt 11:25)

In order to mature spiritually I must know God my Father experientially. Intellectual knowledge does not satisfy the longing in my heart, nor does it beget a loving response to the outpouring of his love. Heart knowledge comes to me only by listening with all my heart to my Father speaking to me.

Jesus, keep my heart simple so that the Father may continue to reveal himself to me.

20 *Do nothing from selfishness or conceit, but in humility count others better than yourselves. Let each of you look not only to his own interests, but also to the interests of others.* (Phil 2:3-4)

I am living in a competitive world. I am told I must succeed at all costs, even if it means ignoring the needs of my neighbor.

Jesus' standards are so different—go the extra mile, offer the other cheek, be reconciled with your brother before offering your gift (see Mt 5:23, 39, 41).

This kind of attitude will not go unnoticed, for Jesus says: "By this all men will know that you are my disciples, if you have love for one another" (Jn 13:35).

21 *"I am not worthy to have you come under my roof."* (Lk 7:6)

These memorable words of the centurion should be my watchword. Jesus comes to me not because I am worthy but because he loves me and cannot separate himself from me and my needs.

Jesus was amazed and pleased at the great faith of the centurion. He was also impressed by his humility and his love for his servant.

Jesus wants to continue his healing in my life. If only I would recognize that he has the power to heal and that in his great love he *wants* to heal—he is just waiting for me to ask him.

22 *"If you would be perfect, go, sell what you possess and give to the poor, and you will have treasure in heaven; and come, follow me."* (Mt 19:21)

What a vulnerable spot Jesus touched when he gave me this directive. I have so many attachments; I am concerned about getting ahead and preparing for the future.

Jesus wants me to enjoy the gifts he gave me but he also wants me to use them for his honor and glory, and only therein will I find happiness and peace.

Furthermore, I cannot follow him if I am weighed down with the excess baggage of worldly interests and possessions.

What can I give away today?

23 *I bid every one among you not to think of himself more highly than he ought to think, but to think with sober judgment, each according to the measure of faith which God has assigned him.*

(Rom 12:3)

Pride is my major failing. I am easily hurt or insulted when I am misunderstood or passed by. I often boast of my prowess or accomplishments, and all because I am really so insecure. Humility is the virtue opposed to pride. Humility is the truth about myself and the truth about God. Without him I can do nothing, but with him I can do all things.

Jesus, help me to remember: "Whoever exalts himself will be humbled, and whoever humbles himself will be exalted" (Mt 23:12).

24 *"Whoever receives one such child in my name receives me; and whoever receives me, receives not me but him who sent me."* (Mk 9:37)

A child is the epitome of goodness, innocence, dependence, humility, and simplicity. Jesus reveals and reflects these same attitudes in his personality. By encouraging me to become like a child, Jesus is really asking me to become like him, to become more Christlike.

I am created in the image and likeness of God, and as I accept the lovable characteristics of a little child I am conforming more and more to God's image.

25 *"Come to me, all who labor and are heavy laden, and I will give you rest."* (Mt 11:28)

A proud person strives to assert his independence and pretends that he does not have to rely on anyone. On the other hand, a humble person will recognize his dependence on others and be truly grateful to them.

Jesus wants me to recognize my total dependence on him. His invitation so gracious and gentle, his promise is so reassuring.

Jesus, thank you for constantly refreshing me when I come to you in humility.

26 *God chose what is foolish in the world to shame the wise, God chose what is weak in the world to shame the strong.* (1 Cor 1:27)

Bernadette of Lourdes, the children at Fatima, St. John Vianney, and Pope John XXIII are only a few of those God chose to bring the Good News to a desolate world. Most likely, they would not have been my first choices for such an important mission.

God also chose me, with all my limitations, shortcomings, hang-ups, and weaknesses, to be a member of his family and to radiate his divine life and love to others.

If I am weak, then he is strong; and did he not say: My ways are not your ways (see Is 55:9)?

27 *"Let the children come to me, and do not hinder them; for to such belongs the kingdom of heaven."* (Mt 19:14)

Little children are helpless and vulnerable. They must depend on those who love them for their survival.

Little children reach out with confidence and trust to those who love them. They are like sponges soaking up all the attention and love which is offered.

Jesus wants little children to learn that he loves them with a providing, caring, concerned, enduring love.

Jesus reminds me that I, like a child, must reach out to him with confidence and trust.

28 *"Truly, truly, I say to you, a servant is not greater than his master; nor is he who is sent greater than he who sent him."* (Jn 13:16)

Sometimes it seems hard for me to take a backseat, to listen to someone talking endlessly without being able to express my own opinions, to have others preferred over me—the litany could go on.

At such moments I need to recall that Jesus was born in a cattle shed—helpless, vulnerable. He hugged lepers, washed the feet of his disciples, permitted himself to be a victim of the atrocities of his enemies.

Dare I expect to be treated better than my Master?

29 *"[God] who is mighty has done great things for me, and holy is his name." (Lk 1:49)*

Mary was truly humble; she honestly admitted that all ages would call her blessed. Her humility radiated itself when she said: "God who is mighty has done great things for me."

Mary was a willing instrument in God's salvific plan. She gave herself totally to the Lord when she announced: "Behold, I am the handmaid of the Lord; let it be to me according to your word."

30 *[Jesus] emptied himself, taking the form of a servant, being born in the likeness of men. (Phil 2:7)*

Jesus divested himself of all his divine prerogatives in order to redeem me. By his total emptying, he mapped out the way for me to follow.

I, too, must forget all my selfish ambitions, my lofty ideas, my grandiose endeavors which do not lead me into a closer relationship with my Father in heaven.

Lord, take my hand and lead me down the road you traveled.

31 *But the meek shall possess the land, and delight themselves in abundant prosperity. (Ps 37:11)*

Jesus was the most peaceful person who ever lived, because he was the personification of meekness. He wants to share his peace with me; hence he bade me: "Learn from me; for I am gentle and lowly in heart" (Mt 11:29).

If I strive to be "gentle and lowly in heart" in imitation of

Jesus, then I shall "delight in abundant prosperity."

And the land I shall possess, according to his promise, is the kingdom of heaven. What more could I ask?

To Hunger and Thirst for Holiness

Blessed are those who hunger and thirst for righteousness, for they shall be satisfied.

MATTHEW 5:6

T he Lord wants each one of us to be a holy person—open and receptive to his divine life and love. He wants to "fill" us now and for all eternity.

Holiness is a gift from God. For our part we must be vessels wide open to receiving the outpouring of his "living water." The extent of our receptivity will determine how much Jesus will be able to form and transform us into holy persons.

Please God, as we listen to your Word in the scriptural passages which follow, intensify our hunger and thirst for you, and fill us with your divine life and love.

1 *"Blessed are those who hunger and thirst for righteousness, for they shall be satisfied."* (Mt 5:6)

I seem to have a built-in longing to know God better as my loving Father. I want him to love me and I want to experience his love. My life is exciting and challenging because I don't know what he will ask of me in the next hour.

Father, only you can give me the fulfillment for which I am longing. Bless me, Lord, with an awareness of your love today.

2 *Seek the Lord while he may be found, call upon him while he is near.* (Is 55:6)

My loving Father says: "You will seek me and find me; when you seek me with all your heart" (Jer 29:13).

The Lord is never far away; he is always present to me. My concern is to keep myself aware of his abiding presence always with me.

Lord, let me walk with you today as I know you are walking with me.

3 *"For I tell you, unless your righteousness exceeds that of the scribes and Pharisees, you will never enter the kingdom of heaven."* (Mt 5:20)

The scribes and Pharisees were formal religionists. While they observed the most minute details of the Law, their motives were questionable.

God looks at the intentions of my heart. If I am trying to love God, he accepts my efforts as love; if I aim to serve him, he is pleased. Whatever I do accomplish is his gift to me. My gift to him is a willingness to respond to the desire he gives me, and that will admit me into his kingdom.

4 *Receive with meekness the implanted word, which is able to save your souls.* (Jas 1:21)

Jesus is present in his Word. His presence gives his Word power. As I spend time listening to his Word in prayer, it will find a home in my heart and will take root there.

Whether or not I am aware of it, his Word will effect a great transformation within me. I will be putting on the new nature. I will be radiating the mind and heart of Jesus by my attitudes and actions.

His Word will also move me into a deeper union with him.

5 *Jesus said to them, "Render to Caesar the things that are Caesar's, and to God the things that are God's."* (Mk 12:17)

God blessed me with a superabundance of gifts to be used in various ways. Too much attachment to incidentals will distract me from the attention I should be giving to God—my one priority.

Let go and let Caesar have what is his.

6 *Set your minds on things that are above, not on things that are on earth.* (Col 3:2)

When I am driving along the highway I must keep my eyes on the road if I hope to reach my destination safely. Similarly, if I am seeking holiness I must keep my attention on the Lord.

Father, on my pilgrimage back to you, help me observe and obey the road signs which guide me to my final destiny.

7 *"Every one who comes to me and hears my words and does them."* (Lk 6:47)

Jesus, your Word is so close to me I can hold it in my hand. You are present in your Word. Give me the generosity to spend some time each day listening to what you are saying to me.

I know your Word has the power to transform me if I let it find a home in my heart (see Jn 15:3; Heb 4:12).

8 *Jesus answered her, "If you knew the gift of God, and who it is that is saying to you, 'Give me a drink,' you would have asked him, and he would have given you living water."* (Jn 4:10)

I get thirsty often during the day, and I always enjoy pausing to share a drink with someone. Jesus, you promised to quench my spiritual thirst with living water—your divine life and love.

Jesus, let us sit down together and enjoy your living water, which alone satisfies my thirst for you. And keep me thirsting for more.

9 *"Truly, truly, I say to you, unless a grain of wheat falls into the earth and dies, it remains alone; but if it dies, it bears much fruit."* (Jn 12:24)

How picturesquely, yet how profoundly, Jesus explains the essential attitude for growing in holiness. Just as a single grain of wheat must die to itself before it can produce an abundant harvest, so I must constantly die to self so that I might be filled with God's life and love. As I empty myself, he fills me with himself.

Only he can produce a harvest in me.

10 *"I am the bread of life; he who comes to me shall not hunger."* (Jn 6:35)

Just as a growing teenager is always hungry, so I should constantly hunger for a deeper relationship with Jesus. He feeds me in the Eucharist and promises that he will fill my hunger. The more I permit his divine life to flourish within me, the more fulfilled my life will be.

This is why Jesus says to me: "I have earnestly desired to eat this passover with you" (Lk 22:15).

11 *Do not be conformed to this world but be transformed by the renewal of your mind, that you may prove what is the will of God, what is good and acceptable and perfect.* (Rom 12:2)

In this age of environmental consciousness I am kept constantly aware of the dangers of air pollution. With twenty-five thousand respirations each day, I can imbibe much toxic air.

Similarly, spiritual pollution envelops me on all sides and is even more hazardous. I must breathe in the divine life which Jesus shares with me to avoid being poisoned by the polluted, godless atmosphere about me.

Lord, let me breathe in your divine life with every breath, and may it counteract whatever dangers threaten me.

12

God is at work in you, both to will and to work for his good pleasure. (Phil 2:13)

All too often I promise God the heroic things I am going to accomplish for him. Sometimes I think he "mischievously" lets me fail and fall on my face to remind me that my very desire to serve him is his gift to me. All he asks of me is to be open to receive this gift of desire as well as the further graces of strength and perseverance needed to fulfill it.

Once again I am reminded that Jesus meant it when he said: "Apart from me you can do nothing" (Jn 15:5).

13

Brethren, do not be weary in well-doing. (2 Thes 3:13)

I am reminded in God's Word that he who perseveres until the end will be saved. Nevertheless, much of my life can become routine and monotonous even while I am striving to do what is right.

The solution: time spent in listening prayer each day will give me the motivation and inspiration I need to keep on the ball.

14

Put on the new nature, created after the likeness of God in true righteousness and holiness. (Eph 4:24)

When a potter finishes his work a whole new form emerges from the lump of clay.

I must be clay in the divine Potter's hands. Only when I spend time resting in his hands can he mold, shape, and transform me into the kind of person he wants me to be.

Lord, make me a new and different person. Keep me pliable in your hands.

15 *Be steadfast, immovable, always abounding in the work of the Lord, knowing that in the Lord your labor is not in vain.*
(1 Cor 15:58)

When I am inclined to become discouraged, I must remember that discouragement is the favorite tool of the evil one.

On the other hand, the grace of perseverance is God's special gift to aid me in being steadfast in my daily duties.

My desire is to do everything for God's honor and glory; he does not judge success or failure as I would. My loving Father sees my heart and knows my intentions.

16 *"Go, sell what you have, and give to the poor, and you will have treasure in heaven; and come, follow me."* (Mk 10:21)

This man loved Jesus and wanted to be his disciple. Jesus loved him too. But the man went away sad because he was very much attached to his wealth and found the conditions for being Jesus' disciple too hard.

I may not be rich, but there are many other little tin or neon gods which dominate my life and prevent me from following Jesus more closely. Jesus, let me look at them objectively, and don't let me go away sad. How much have I given to the poor during this past month? How much of my time have I given to others?

17 *"He who is of God hears the words of God."* (Jn 8:47)

I must keep my antenna pointed God-ward if I want to stay in touch with you, Jesus. In these words, you are reminding me that I must always remain tuned in if I am to hear what you are saying to me.

Your Father urged me to be receptive when he said: "Listen to him" (Lk 9:35).

Lord, give me a listening heart, that I might be molded and transformed by your Word.

18 *"And as for that in the good soil, they are those who, hearing the word, hold it fast in an honest and good heart, and bring forth fruit with patience."* (Lk 8:15)

What a picturesque image Jesus gives me in this parable! The seed of his Word has an unlimited potential; I must be receptive to it and allow it to take root within me.

I must care for it, nurture it, water it, keep it exposed to the sun. The time I spend in prayer provides this tender care for the seed of God's Word.

Lord, may I treasure those precious times with you in prayer.

19 *"To serve him in holiness and virtue in his presence, all our days."* (Lk 1:75, JB)

As I pray Zechariah's canticle I am reminded that I must serve God devoutly. Such a life of service must be motivated by love, and the degree of my love for God can be measured by my love for others.

When I am lovingly concerned about others, when I am selflessly interested in their welfare, then I am growing in holiness.

Today, Lord, let me prove my love by a special act of concern for some person you send across my path.

20 *"Teacher, what shall I do to inherit eternal life?"* (Lk 10:25)

When the lawyer expressed his desire for holiness Jesus pointed to the love of neighbor as the ideal way. Jesus told him the story of the Good Samaritan. The Good Samaritan did what I would expect done for me in the same circumstances.

I am reminded of the Golden Rule Jesus enunciated: "Treat others the way you would have them treat you."

Jesus, today let me be aware of the little ways I can reach out in love to my neighbor.

21 *He has showed you, O man, what is good; and what does the Lord require of you but to do justice, and to love kindness, and to walk humbly with your God?* (Mi 6:8)

These words remind me of the two disciples on the road to Emmaus. They walked humbly with Jesus; they listened; finally they recognized him.

Jesus walks with me each day. If I listen humbly, I will know what he is asking of me at that moment. As I listen my journey becomes a joyous, fulfilling experience.

My journey's end will bring me into the arms of my Father.

22 *[God] chose us in him before the foundation of the world, that we should be holy and blameless before him.* (Eph 1:4)

God chose me even before I was born—from all eternity. He called me to follow the way Jesus mapped out for me, especially the directives given in the Beatitudes. Jesus lived the Beatitudes perfectly.

Jesus bids me to "come and see" and then he says, "Follow me."

I am special to God. He predestined me and adopted me. What a challenge for me to live up to my calling—"to be holy and blameless in his sight."

23 *"You, therefore, must be perfect, as your heavenly Father is perfect."* (Mt 5:48)

Only when I do all in my power to love and to forgive others can Jesus living in me reach out to others through me. Jesus made this a requirement for growth in holiness. I am to be his chosen channel.

Then I will be striving to "be perfect." This is my way to holiness. This is what my heavenly Father expects of me.

Jesus, you are the Way. Keep me on that Way as you lead me to the Father.

24 *"But I say to you, Love your enemies and pray for those who persecute you, so that you may be sons of your Father who is in heaven; for he makes his sun rise on the evil and on the good, and sends rain on the just and on the unjust."* (Mt 5:44-45)

Jesus expects me to love not only my friends, but also those who hate me. My heavenly Father loves both the good and the bad. He provides sunshine and rain which produce a rich harvest for all without distinction.

If I am to be a child of my heavenly Father, I must love in this same way. I may not be aware of hating anyone, but if I am indifferent or apathetic to a person, or if I lack a loving concern for someone, then I am not loving as Jesus loves.

Lord, help me love others as you love me.

25 *"Let him who is thirsty come, let him who desires take the water of life without price."* (Rv 22:17)

I know the pain and agony of a parched throat and the craving for a drink of soothing cool water.

Terrible as this desire may be, it cannot be compared with my hunger and thirst for God's love. As I come to know Jesus more and more, this desire will never be satisfied until I am closely united with him.

Jesus, you are the life-giving water. Fill my heart to the brim with your divine life and love.

26 *As a hart longs for flowing streams, so longs my soul for thee, O God. My soul thirsts for God, for the living God.*
(Ps 42:1-2)

I once observed several deer coming toward a gorgeous waterfall in the woods. Usually deer are extremely cautious and careful not to be detected, but this day they seemed to throw caution to the wind as they rushed to the refreshing stream of water near the falls.

These animals taught me a valuable lesson. If my soul is really thirsting for the Lord, if I honestly desire to be closely united with him, I should forge ahead, disregarding those many things which often impede my progress: the opinions of others, temporal concerns, the many inhibitions which plague me and which shackle my progress on my way to the Father.

27 *To do righteousness and justice is more acceptable to the Lord than sacrifice.* (Prv 21:3)

At times I am deeply concerned about *doing* things for the Lord. I am solicitous about my devotional practices. I want to prove my love for the Lord by doing something very special for him.

All this is commendable, but what Jesus is asking of me is simply to *be* for him, to let him love me; to rest and relax in the sunshine of his presence and permit him to mold and transform me.

Jesus, I am not accustomed to simply "wasting" time in your presence, but I am begging you to teach me and show me the way.

28 *If we live by the Spirit, let us also walk by the Spirit.* (Gal 5:25)

Since my baptism, the Holy Spirit is dwelling within me; I am his temple. I cannot objectify his presence, but I know he is dynamic and operative within me, motivating, guiding, and strengthening me.

To keep myself alert to his inspirations and directives, I must listen regularly at the very core of my being. This time spent in listening prayer will satisfy the hunger and thirst I have for a deeper walk in holiness.

Come, Holy Spirit, give me a listening heart.

29 *May the God of peace himself sanctify you wholly; and may your spirit and soul and body be kept sound and blameless at the coming of our Lord Jesus Christ.* (1 Thes 5:23)

In this passage what a powerful prayer St. Paul is sending heavenward for me! I am reminded, too, that the whole communion of saints is praying for my spiritual progress. They want me to be united with them in the joy and happiness of heaven. How encouraging to know that I am not walking alone in this land of exile as I journey back to the Father!

What support and encouragement to know that St. Paul and all the heavenly host love me enough to want me with them.

30 *For the grace of God has appeared for the salvation of all men, training us to renounce irreligion and worldly passions, and to live sober, upright, and godly lives in this world.* (Ti 2:11-12)

After his redemptive work was finished, Jesus handed over the accomplishment of my sanctification and the sanctification of all his members to the Holy Spirit.

I am the temple of the Holy Spirit. By his special gifts he is enlightening, guiding, and strengthening me. Above all, he is warming me with his love, giving me the inspiration to respond more generously in loving service.

31 *"Blessed rather are those who hear the Word of God and keep it!"* (Lk 11:28)

In one brief statement Jesus explains to me the way to holiness. God speaks to me through his Word. As I listen to his Word at the very core of my being, a tremendous change is taking place in me.

His Word inspires and motivates me; it turns me away from all that is not God and transforms me more and more into the image of God.

This is true blessedness.

To Be Merciful

Blessed are the merciful, for they shall obtain mercy.

MATTHEW 5:7

Throughout his life Jesus continually reached out with his merciful, compassionate love to the poor and under-privileged, to the suffering and rejected, to everyone who needed him. A disciple follows Jesus so closely that he can be identified with him. His heart must overflow with the same merciful compassion which Jesus manifested.

The Father will dispose our hearts for this apostolate, for he promised: "A new heart I will give you, and a new spirit I will put within you; and I will take out of your flesh the heart of stone and give you a heart of flesh" (Ez 36:26).

In this Beatitude Jesus says: "I am a merciful, compassionate God, and blessed will you be if you show mercy to others."

As we meet Jesus present in his Word in the pages which fol-low, we will conform our hearts according to the pattern of his own loving heart. May he give us a complete heart transplant.

1 *"Blessed are the merciful, for they shall obtain mercy."* (Mt 5:7)

Throughout his earthly sojourn Jesus proved himself to be a loving, merciful, compassionate, and forgiving God. As his follower, he is inviting me to be like him: merciful and compassionate.

When I show mercy to others, I am a blessing to them and I will also be singularly blessed myself.

Lord, help me to reach out in love to someone today.

2 *"Be merciful, even as your Father is merciful."* (Lk 6:36)

My Father in heaven is so merciful that he wants to forgive, heal, and redeem me more than I could ever desire it myself. That is the mystery of God's love.

When Jesus invited me to follow him, he encouraged me to show loving mercy and compassion in all my dealings with others.

As I keep my focus on the compassion of the Father and on the loving mercy of Jesus, I, too, will become more compassionate. Hasten that day, Lord Jesus.

3 *"Judge not, and you will not be judged."* (Lk 6:37a)

When I judge others I reveal my own insecurities and weaknesses. Furthermore, I usurp God's role since he alone knows the heart of man.

Jesus, what a noble example you gave me as you stood silent before your accusers.

4 *"Condemn not, and you will not be condemned."* (Lk 6:37b)

What right have I to condemn another? How can I know his or her motivation or weaknesses or temptations?

The Lord reminds me, "I, the Lord, alone probe the mind and test the heart" (Jer 17:10).

Let me remember: "But for the grace of God, there go I."

5 *"Forgive, and you will be forgiven."* (Lk 6:37c)

When it seems hard to forgive a person, I would do well to go in spirit to Calvary and listen to all the insults, derision, mockery, and blasphemy being hurled at Jesus, and realize that my sins caused some of that cruel treatment.

Above all, I must listen to Jesus' prayer: "Father, forgive them; for they know not what they do" (Lk 23:34). I am included in that prayer.

6 *Forbearing one another.* (Col 3:13a)

My greatest challenge in life is to relate lovingly to all those persons God sends into my life. My own insecurity often makes me judgmental, jealous, critical, and defensive.

If I humbly strive to bear with them, the Lord will not only heal me, but will also help me establish a real bond of love with those persons I once found difficult to love.

"Lord Jesus, you came to reconcile us to one another and to the Father: Lord, have mercy."

7 *Forgiving each other; as the Lord has forgiven you, so you also must forgive.* (Col 3:13b)

Jesus loves me so much that he always forgives me regardless of what I have done. Strange as it may seem, the more graciously I forgive, the happier I will be.

Jesus, forgive me my trespasses as I am trying to forgive those who have trespassed against me.

8 *The Lord is merciful and gracious, slow to anger and abounding in steadfast love.* (Ps 103:8)

At times our impression of God is a distorted one. Often we think of him as a vengeful judge, demanding his "pound of flesh." This picture is certainly not scriptural.

How briefly, yet how beautifully, the psalmist describes God as a merciful and gracious Lord, slow to anger and abounding in kindness.

"Have mercy on me, O God, according to thy steadfast love; according to thy abundant mercy blot out my transgressions" (Ps 51:1).

9 *"Just so, I tell you, there will be more joy in heaven over one sinner who repents than over ninety-nine righteous persons who need no repentance."* (Lk 15:7)

God wants to fill me with his divine love, but when I sin I am saying no to God's love. By repenting I reopen the door to a greater influx of his divine life and love into my life.

There is joy in heaven because my repentance unites me more closely with the whole communion of saints since we form one body with Christ as our Head.

My repentance brings healing to a sinful world.

10 *"Father, forgive them; for they know not what they do."* (Lk 23:34)

Even though his pain was excruciating, Jesus loved enough to reach out in forgiveness.

By my sins I caused some of the pain which Jesus endured. Any pain, rejection, insult, or injury which I suffer cannot be compared with the agony of Jesus. Should I not then reach out in loving compassion?

Jesus, forgive me; for I certainly cannot fathom what I am doing when I sin.

11 *For by grace you have been saved through faith; and this is not your own doing, it is the gift of God—not because of works, lest any man should boast.* (Eph 2:8-9)

Our loving Father knows that I could never save myself. Salvation is his precious gift to me. Furthermore, he desires my salvation more than I myself could ever desire it. His love for me is infinite, and his desire to have me united with him eternally in love is infinite.

Thank you, Father, for that gift. Teach me to long for it, and also to use every means to receive it.

12 *"Those who are well have no need of a physician, but those who are sick. Go and learn what this means, 'I desire mercy, and not sacrifice.' For I came not to call the righteous, but sinners."*

(Mt 9:12-13)

How welcome the healing touch of a physician when I am ill! How eager I am to be relieved of pain and suffering!

Jesus came to relieve and heal me of all spiritual ills by bringing me peace and pardon.

To be his disciple, I must be willing to extend that same mercy to others.

13 *"Let him who is without sin among you be the first to throw a stone at her."* (Jn 8:7)

How easy to point my finger at another person and project my own guilt onto that person!

Thank you, Jesus, for reminding me to look at my own record. Even a casual glance at it will cause me to lay down my stone.

14 *Let all bitterness and wrath and anger and clamor and slander be put away from you, with all malice, and be kind to one another, tenderhearted, forgiving one another, as God in Christ forgave you.* (Eph 4:31-32)

St. Paul is quite imperative when he states how a follower of Jesus must be, but he is only reiterating what Jesus himself taught by word and by example.

Jesus, enlighten me as I ponder each word of this admonition, and assist me in translating it into practice in my daily living.

15 *"So if you are offering your gift at the altar, and there remember that your brother has something against you, leave your gift there before the altar and go; first be reconciled to your brother, and then come and offer your gift."* (Mt 5:23-24)

Jesus is reminding me that my interior disposition is of paramount importance when I come to participate in the Holy Eucharist. How readily I harbor little hurts and bruises—even, at times, some bitterness or resentment.

Jesus, when my pride is wounded, heal me so that I can forgive and be more like you.

16 *Jesus in pity touched their eyes, and immediately they received their sight and followed him.* (Mt 20:34)

My self-centeredness keeps my vision so myopic. Jesus, touch me and heal me so I can see you more clearly and follow you more closely.

Open my eyes and broaden my vision so I can recognize you in everyone I meet today.

17 *"If you forgive men their trespasses, your heavenly Father also will forgive you."* (Mt 6:14)

When I refuse to forgive others, I am setting up all sorts of roadblocks and obstacles to the loving mercy and compassion of my forgiving Father.

On the other hand, when I forgive others, I make myself more and more receptive to the abundance of God's mercy and forgiveness.

18 *"I am He who blots out your transgressions for my own sake, and I will not remember your sins."* (Is 43:25)

How could God say that he wants to wipe out my sins for his own sake? He loves me with an infinite, immutable love. And love must give.

Forgiveness originates with him; how greatly he wants to extend to me his forgiving, forgetting touch.

What joy and consolation your words bring.

19 *Judgment is without mercy to one who has shown no mercy; yet mercy triumphs over judgment.* (Jas 2:13)

God understands my human weakness. He knows how hard it is for me to forgive and how much harder it is for me to forget. But Jesus showed me the way. His whole lifetime was one continuous reaching-out in mercy and compassion—to the poor and underprivileged; to the suffering and rejected; in a word, to everyone. A disciple follows the Master so closely that he can be identified with him. If I am of goodwill Jesus will endow me with the grace necessary to follow in his footsteps.

"Where sin increased, grace abounded all the more" (Rom 5:20).

20 *"My heavenly Father will do to every one of you, if you do not forgive your brother from your heart." (Mt 18:35)*

To forgive from the heart means that I must forgive without any recriminations. I must not give the impression that I am doing the person a favor by forgiving him or her.

To forgive from the heart means furthermore that I must be willing to forget the whole matter. That can be very difficult at times.

Lord, you have forgiven me more frequently than I could calculate. Teach me to forgive and forget.

21 *"Lord, how often shall my brother sin against me, and I forgive him? As many as seven times?" Jesus said to him, "I do not say to you seven times, but seventy times seven." (Mt 18:21-22)*

Jesus is saying that there is no limit to how often I must forgive others. The offenses I suffer are often unintentional on the other person's part, and insignificant compared to my infidelities toward God and others.

I must forgive if I wish to be forgiven. In the Our Father, Jesus teaches me not only to pray for forgiveness, but also to ask for the grace that enables me to forgive others.

The more I show mercy, the more I will be a true disciple of Jesus.

22 *If we confess our sins, he is faithful and just, and will forgive our sins and cleanse us from all unrighteousness.* (1 Jn 1:9)

Jesus wants to purify me but I must be willing to receive the influx of his forgiving, healing, and redeeming love. By my openness to receive his mercy, I express my love for him, my Savior and Redeemer.

I need to recall many times what Jesus said: "Her sins, which are many, are forgiven, for she loved much; but he who is forgiven little, loves little" (Lk 7:47).

Jesus' merciful love does not change; but as I love more intensely, I am able to imbibe more of his love.

23 *"Lord, do not hold this sin against them."* (Acts 7:60)

Stephen was a true disciple of Jesus. He had absorbed the mind and heart of Jesus to such an extent that he could forgive his murderers. Martyrs down through the ages have joyously forgiven their executioners and thus given even greater witness to the love of Jesus radiating through them.

My martyrdoms are insignificant compared to what these heroes of Christ have suffered. Can I honestly say with Jesus: "Father, forgive them; for they know not what they do" (Lk 23:34)? Or with St. Stephen: "Lord, do not hold this sin against them"?

24 *We exhort you, brethren, admonish the idlers, encourage the fainthearted, help the weak, be patient with them all.*
(1 Thes 5:14)

Jesus reflected his mercy and compassion at every moment during his public ministry. He forgave sins; he healed broken bodies and spirits; he brought comfort and consolation, peace and joy to weary hearts. He says to me: "I have given you an example, that you also should do as I have done to you" (Jn 13:15).

Alexander Pope prayed for this disposition in The Universal Prayer: "Teach me to feel another's woe, To hide the fault I see; That mercy I to others show, That mercy show to me."

25 *But God, who is rich in mercy, out of the great love with which he loved us, even when we were dead through our trespasses, made us alive together with Christ (by grace you have been saved).*
(Eph 2:4-5)

I am often plagued with the thought that when I sin, God may forgive me *if* I fulfill certain conditions—if I am sorry for my sin, if I resolve to avoid it, if I am willing to make reparation, *then* God may condescend to forgive me. These dispositions of mind and heart are essential, but my conclusion does not follow. God is rich in mercy because of his great love; hence he is even more eager and anxious to forgive than I am to be forgiven.

My Father does not desire the death of a sinner, but that he be converted and live.

26 *"I tell you, there will be more joy in heaven over one sinner who repents than over ninety-nine righteous persons who need no repentance."* (Lk 15:7)

Jesus came into the world to be my Savior and Redeemer. It brings him joy each time I ask his mercy on my sinfulness, for I am giving him the opportunity to fulfill his role as Savior in my life. This joy penetrates the heights of heaven, as Jesus tells me.

Furthermore, when I seek his pardon and forgiveness I bring a healing blessing to his Body. Even though I am only an infinitesimal cell in it, my healing touches the whole Body.

27 *My heart recoils within me, my compassion grows warm and tender.* (Hos 11:8)

When I contemplate God's forgiving mercy and compassion for me, a sinner, my heart, too, is overwhelmed by the mystery of his love for me in spite of my infidelity.

When I sin I refuse to respond to his love for me. This realization brings me to a sincere sorrow. How can I continue to say no to his love?

Father, keep my heart open to the outpouring of your love so that sin will find no place in me.

28 *By this we know love, that he laid down his life for us; and we ought to lay down our lives for the brethren.* (1 Jn 3:16)

Jesus himself said that there is no greater love than for a person to lay down his life for another. Jesus not only redeemed me by his loving mercy and compassion; he asks me to radiate his redemptive love in my personal relationships with all those he sends into my life.

As I accept his forgiveness and love and reach out in mercy and forgiveness to others, I will be singularly blessed.

29 *"Therefore I tell you, her sins, which are many, are forgiven, for she loved much; but he who is forgiven little, loves little."*

(Lk 7:47)

As Jesus journeyed through his public ministry he continuously poured out his mercy and compassion on all in need. He continues that same ministry today. Daily he is enveloping me with his healing, forgiving love.

His love flows in superabundance, but how much I receive depends upon my receptivity. When I strive to love much, his forgiveness will be superabundant.

Lord, have mercy.

30 *The Lord is merciful and gracious, slow to anger and abounding in steadfast love.* (Ps 103:8)

The loving mercy and tender compassion of God is a constantly recurring theme in the Psalms. It is repeated so frequently because I need to be reminded of the Father's forgiving, healing love.

"To err is human, to forgive is divine."

Too often I dwell on only the first part of this maxim; God's desire to forgive is beyond my human comprehension.

Lord, teach me the blessedness of being merciful in all my dealings with others.

31 *Give thanks to the Lord, for he is good, for his steadfast love endures for ever.* (Ps 136)

In this psalm the sacred writer reminds me twenty-six times that my loving Father's mercy will endure forever, regardless of what I have done or will do.

As my Good Shepherd, his "goodness and mercy shall follow me all the days of my life" (Ps 23:6).

My heart rejoices at such extravagant goodness and kindness. I want to shout with joy for such incomprehensible love for me.

What else could I ask, except a loving heart in return?

To Be Single-Hearted

Blessed are the pure in heart, for they shall see God.

MATTHEW 5:8

M oses reminds us: "For the Lord your God is a devouring fire, a jealous God" (Dt 4:24). He wants our undivided heart and efforts always directed toward him and his holy will for us. God is not a selfish God simply desiring our set purpose in life to be directed toward him for his own sake. On the contrary, God knows that single-heartedness is the only avenue to a joyful, happy, peaceful life.

Enjoying life to the full with this mind-set will give great glory to our loving Father and assure us of "seeing God."

The brief scriptural passages for each day of this month should help us follow Christ to be single-hearted.

1 *"Blessed are the pure in heart, for they shall see God."* (Mt 5:8)

In effect Jesus is saying in this Beatitude: "I am pure in heart, and blessed will you be if you strive to be pure in heart as I am. Then you will truly be my follower and a devoted disciple."

Lord Jesus, help me to rid myself of all the tinsel which would divert me and lead me off on a tangent away from you and my set purpose in life.

2 *"Did you not know that I must be in my Father's house?"* (Lk 2:49)

Even at the early age of twelve Jesus had his focus on only one objective: doing the will of the Father. In spite of the fact that it caused some pain to Mary and Joseph, the Father held first priority in Jesus' life.

Jesus, help me to put aside all human considerations, that I may know and fulfill your will in my life.

3 *"If you keep my commandments, you will abide in my love, just as I have kept my Father's commandments and abide in his love."* (Jn 15:10)

Keeping Jesus' commandments is not primarily a matter of obeying rules and regulations; rather, it is living in the Spirit of Jesus—having his mind in me.

It means being single-hearted, as Jesus was, in doing the will of the Father. Jesus not only taught me the way, but he *is the way*.

Living in his love means letting him fill me with his life and love.

4 *"Where your treasure is, there will your heart be also." (Lk 12:34)*

How easily and tenaciously my heart clings to doing what I want! I want to control, to accomplish my own ends—sometimes with a total disregard for others' wishes and needs.

Jesus, teach me to say: "Thy will be done." Keep my heart on the right track.

5 *We receive from him whatever we ask, because we keep his commandments and do what pleases him. (1 Jn 3:22)*

If I am doing what is pleasing in God's sight, then I will ask only those things which will enable me to walk ever more deeply in his love. How delighted God will be to grant these petitions because this is what he wants for me!

"Your heavenly Father knows that you need them all" (Mt 6:32).

6 *So, whether you eat or drink, or whatever you do, do all to the glory of God. (1 Cor 10:31)*

Nothing I do in life, regardless of how insignificant it may appear, is unimportant to God. As my gracious Father he is interested in everything I do.

However, he is more concerned about *why* I do everything than *what* I do. My disposition, my attitude, my motivation for doing something is vitally important.

"Blest are the single-hearted!"

7 *It is no longer I who live, but Christ who lives in me.* (Gal 2:20)

The more I become aware of Jesus dwelling within me, the more my thoughts and attitudes will become like his.

His divine indwelling will bring me much peace and joy because my personal resurrection will have already begun.

Jesus, how encouraging to know that you and the Father will come to me and make your dwelling place with me (Jn 14:23).

8 *"I can do nothing on my own authority ... but the will of him who sent me."* (Jn 5:30)

How frequently Jesus reminds me that his Father's will was the all-important factor in his life! Everything else was secondary.

Jesus, help me to say: "Here I am, Lord, what is it you want of me today?"

9 *My eyes are ever toward the Lord.* (Ps 25:15)

One of the first rules of golf is to keep my eye on the ball. Even a momentary glance up could ruin my swing and cost me extra strokes.

Similarly, a turning away from the Lord could cause me to go off on a tangent. Keeping "my eyes ever toward the Lord" will keep me on course, and all else will become peripheral.

10 *"Whoever does the will of my Father in heaven is my brother, and sister, and mother."* (Mt 12:50)

Jesus is telling me that my spiritual relationship with him is far more important than any family ties. When I live according to his way, the Father adopts me as his child. I become an heir of God and an heir with Christ (see Rom 8:17).

I become a member of God's royal family. What a privilege! What a dignity!

11 *Finally, brethren, whatever is true, whatever is honorable, whatever is just, whatever is pure, whatever is lovely, whatever is gracious, if there is any excellence, if there is anything worthy of praise, think about these things.* (Phil 4:8)

When my focus is on Jesus, when I spend time regularly with him in prayer, when he becomes the number one priority in my life, then a great conversion takes place within me.

My self-centeredness will be gradually changed into a Christ-centeredness. When Jesus becomes the center of my life, I will experience true peace and joy.

12 *I delight to do thy will, O my God; thy law is within my heart.* (Ps 40:8)

The first concern in the life of Jesus was to do his Father's will. If I am to be his follower, this must become my first concern also.

First, in my daily duties I must want to do the will of God; secondly, to do it in the manner he wills; and thirdly, to do it *because* it is his will.

13 *"You are my friends if you do what I command you."*
(Jn 15:14)

A friend is a person I admire, esteem, and love. Jesus accepts and loves me as a very special friend. If I really cherish his friendship, I will want to do what is pleasing to him.

He asks me to do nothing which is not for my own personal growth in holiness and spiritual maturity.

Jesus, let me listen intently as you say to me: "I have called you friends" (Jn 15:15).

14 *"Blest are those who hear the word of God and keep it."*
(Lk 11:28)

Jesus is present in his Word. When I listen to his Word, I am listening to Jesus personally. When his Word finds a home in my heart, I am permitting Jesus to dwell in me and be more fully operative within me.

Then I will be singularly blest because the Father and Jesus will make their home with me (see Jn 14:23).

15 *"He who is of God hears the words of God."* (Jn 8:47)

I am always attentive to those I love. I strive to anticipate their wishes and needs even before they are expressed.

As I try to grow and mature in my love for God, my heart is always eager and anxious to listen to what he wishes to say to me. I find much peace and contentment in giving him my time in a listening posture.

"Speak, Lord, for thy servant hears" (1 Sm 3:9).

16 *"Thy will be done, on earth as it is in heaven."* (Mt 6:10)

If I want to do God's will at all times, I must be willing to stop in the middle of what I am doing and do whatever is asked of me.

Lord, help me to recognize your will, and give me the strength to do it.

17 *For to me to live is Christ, and to die is gain.* (Phil 1:21)

How truly St. Paul has spoken! Jesus shares his divine life with me here and now in this land of exile. Amid all the happenings of everyday living, I know that Jesus will not leave me, but remains with me.

What comfort and consolation knowing that his divine life and love will embrace me at the moment of death.

18 *This is the confidence which we have in him, that if we ask anything according to his will he hears us.* (1 Jn 5:14)

Our Father is a gracious and generous Abba. He wants to give me everything I need on my journey back to him. This is his great desire: to shower his gifts and blessings upon me.

I can manifest my gratitude by thanking him and also by using well the gifts he gives me.

"How much more will your Father who is in heaven give good things to those who ask him!" (Mt 7:11).

19

Therefore do not be foolish, but understand what the will of the Lord is. (Eph 5:17)

Doing God's will brings me peace of mind and heart. Any lack of peace is a red flag warning me that what I am doing, or proposing to do, may not be God's will for me at this time.

When I love a person, I have an innate sense of what that person wishes me to do. The more I love the Lord, the easier it will be for me to know what he wants of me in any given situation.

O Holy Spirit, endow me with the "ability to distinguish between spirits" (1 Cor 12:10).

20

He who loves his brother abides in the light, and in it there is no cause for stumbling. (1 Jn 2:10)

If I am faithful in staying close to Jesus the Light, he will teach me not only how to love my brothers and sisters, but he will love them for me and through me. I must remain adamant in walking with him.

Love will enable me to avoid many sins. If I do sin, I have the assurance that "love covers a multitude of sins" (1 Pt 4:8).

Jesus, keep me single-hearted as you were.

21 *"As the Father has loved me, so have I loved you; abide in my love."* (Jn 15:9)

What a gracious invitation Jesus extends to me: to live in the sunshine of his love, to be warmed and cherished by his love, to be nourished and strengthened by his love.

How generous is the Father's promise to me: "My steadfast love shall not depart from you, and my covenant of peace shall not be removed" (Is 54:10).

Surely the Lord is single-hearted in doing everything to bring me happiness in this land of exile as a prelude to that happiness which awaits me in the kingdom.

22 *"In him we live and move and have our being."* (Acts 17:28)

I am never alone on my journey through life. Jesus is living with me and within me. He is closer to me than the oxygen which not only envelops me but which penetrates my whole being in the process of inhalation.

Jesus is the source of my life. Without him I can do nothing. With him I shall live for all eternity.

On my journey, I must *let* him be my strength.

23 *Do all things without grumbling or questioning, that you may be blameless and innocent, children of God without blemish in the midst of a crooked and perverse generation, among whom you shine as lights in the world.* (Phil 2:14-15)

St. Paul himself was always steadfast and single-hearted in his ministry of spreading the good news of salvation. In this pastoral admonition he encourages me to the same steadfastness, so that, like the stars, I may brighten the path for others.

I will find the source of my strength in the presence of the Lord in his Word.

24 *"I tell you, among those born of women none is greater than John."* (Lk 7:28)

John's greatness consisted in his single-hearted effort to preach the necessity of repentance in preparation for the coming of the kingdom. He persevered in this resolve even though it cost him his head.

Jesus asks me to persevere in following him regardless of the criticism, misunderstanding, and even persecution which I may suffer. This single-heartedness will be my witness to those who hesitate to follow him or to even listen to his Word.

25 *"Truly, I say to you, as you did it to one of the least of these my brethren, you did it to me."* (Mt 25:40)

The Lord offers many opportunities each day for me to love my neighbor as myself. At times I experience personal satisfaction in doing so. At other times I may feel others are taking advantage of me, or that I am being used.

In order to remain faithful and single-hearted in touching others with his love, I must remember that I am doing it for Jesus personally.

Let his words echo in my heart: "You did it to me."

26 *Rejoice in your hope, be patient in tribulation, be constant in prayer.* (Rom 12:12)

When the Lord is my goal in life, when I am single-minded in striving for a deeper relationship with him, I will always find hope, come what may.

I will be a cheerful person even under trial. My joy will automatically radiate to those who cross my path.

The secret of persevering in this endeavor is time spent in prayer. In prayer I meet Jesus and together we can face the pain and enjoy the consolation that life brings.

27 *"And as for that in the good soil, they are those who, hearing the word, hold it fast in an honest and good heart, and bring forth fruit with patience."* (Lk 8:15)

In the realm of nature God provides the seed with its potential and all the climatic conditions necessary to produce a rich harvest. In the spiritual realm he shares his divine life with me and gives me all the gifts and graces I need to nurture it.

For my part I must be open to receiving the outpouring of his life and love. I must care for it, watch it grow and mature, and rejoice at the miracle of life and growth as it produces a rich harvest.

I must let his Word find a home in me, and it will show me the way.

28 *"Father, if thou art willing, remove this cup from me; nevertheless not my will, but thine, be done."* (Lk 22:42)

This was the greatest human decision ever made. In spite of being faced with the most shameful and most painful kind of execution, Jesus wanted to do his Father's will.

Jesus, give me the strength and courage to say my "yes" to the Father in times of suffering.

29 *Blessed is the man who endures trial, for when he has stood the test he will receive the crown of life which God has promised to those who love him.* (Jas 1:12)

Life is a series of hills and valleys. The road through life is sometimes smooth; often it is rough and rocky. Jesus prepared me for this.

If I remain single-hearted in accepting the trials and difficulties which arise, I will soon understand that they are really steppingstones into my union with Jesus. Each difficulty is a rung on the ladder of my ascent to him, drawing me closer to "the crown of life the Lord has promised."

Lead me on, Lord, in your love.

30 *Although he was a Son, he learned obedience through what he suffered; and being made perfect he became the source of eternal salvation to all who obey him.* (Heb 5:8-9)

Jesus was determined to obey every iota of the Father's will. By doing so, Jesus gained for me my eternal salvation. He said: "This is the will of him who sent me, that I should lose nothing of all that he has given me, but raise it up at the last day" (Jn 6:39).

This treasure is mine if I, like Jesus, am concerned about doing the Father's will at every moment of my life. Make me single-hearted, Lord.

31 *"I have come to do thy will, O God."* (Heb 10:7)

What joy Jesus' single-heartedness in doing the will of the Father should bring me! Jesus tells me plainly what the will of the Father is: "This is the will of my Father, that every one who sees the Son and believes in him should have eternal life; and I will raise him up at the last day" (Jn 6:40).

What comfort and consolation this trust brings me. My Father wants my eternal happiness even more than I could want it. What overwhelming love!

To Be Peacemakers

Blessed are the peacemakers, for they shall be called sons of God.

MATTHEW 5:9

Our loving Father is a God of peace. Our peace with God was won by the redemptive love of Jesus. The Holy Spirit is now the source and dispenser of the peace which the world cannot give. Peace is the very essence of the kingdom Jesus established.

As followers of Jesus we are called to peace. "Let the peace of Christ rule in your hearts" (Col 3:15).

As disciples of Jesus we are called also to become witnesses of that peace. Paul urges us to be: "eager to maintain the unity of the Spirit in the bond of peace" (Eph 4:3). As peace reigns in our hearts, our peaceful radiance will draw others into that "bond of peace."

Contemplating the message of the following Scripture passages will augment the peace in our own hearts and transform us into apostolic peacemakers.

1 *"Blessed are the peacemakers, for they shall be called sons of God."*
(Mt 5:9)

As I spend time in prayer—especially the prayer of listening—I will discover a great peace surging through my whole being. The more fully I experience Jesus in my prayer, the more intense will be the peace and joy filling my mind and heart.

I become a peacemaker when I allow the peace and joy of Jesus to radiate through me and touch others.

Listen to Jesus say: "Peace be with you" (Jn 20:21).

2 *Of the increase of his government and of peace there will be no end.* (Is 9:7)

One night I experienced how vast and how peaceful is the Lord's dominion. I walked slowly under a canopy of stars outshone only by the full moon. The birds and neighborhood animals were peacefully resting. The cool evening breeze was refreshing and relaxing. My whole being was filled with quiet peace and joy.

Nature always responds to the Creator's touch, fulfilling his will and purpose perfectly. I, on the other hand, can ignore him or refuse to be docile.

My docility to his plan for me will make his dominion over me peaceful with no end.

3 *Great peace have those who love thy law.* (Ps 119:165)

God's law, his will and wishes, are all embodied in his Person. When I love a person, I want to do what pleases that person. I manifest my love for my gracious Father by desiring to do everything to please him.

The problem is recognizing God's wishes and knowing his will. I can discern God's will for me when I spend time in listening to him and his Word with all my heart.

The more I listen, the better I will know him; and the better I know him, the more I will love him.

4 *Let us then pursue what makes for peace and for mutual upbuilding.* (Rom 14:19)

Peace is God's special gift to me. He bestows this gift upon me so that I may share it with others. In doing so, I will augment the peace of my own heart.

A boundless source of peace is the Mass. In the Mass Jesus unites my prayer with his, making it a powerful prayer of petition. In each Mass I pray with Jesus: "Lord, may this sacrifice, which has made our peace with you, advance the peace and salvation of all the world."

5 *Depart from evil, and do good; seek peace, and pursue it.*
(Ps 34:14)

The inspired psalmist already realized that sin and peace are incompatible. He reminds me to turn away from sin, seek forgiveness, and walk in the way Jesus mapped out so that I might enjoy the peace of the Lord.

By his redemptive and salvific love Jesus won that peace for me; hence at Mass I pray: "Lamb of God, you take away the sins of the world: grant us peace."

6 *May the God of steadfastness and encouragement grant you to live in such harmony with one another, in accord with Christ Jesus.* (Rom 15:5)

The Holy Spirit is the source of unity. Through St. Paul he begs us to live in peace and harmony with one another in order to give witness to the world of the fruits of his divine indwelling: love, peace, and joy.

At Mass we implore the Holy Spirit in our prayer: "Grant that we, who are nourished by his body and blood, may be filled with his Holy Spirit, and become one body, one spirit in Christ."

7 *For he [Jesus] is our peace.* (Eph 2:14)

Jesus willingly laid down his life to redeem me and a sinful world. He is therefore the source of my peace. In each Mass I pray with the priest not only for peace in this life, but a peace which will endure throughout eternity.

Lord Jesus Christ, you said to your apostles: "I leave you peace, my peace I give you." Look not on our sins, but on the faith of your Church and grant us the peace and unity of your kingdom where you live forever and ever. Amen.

8 *"Glory to God in the highest, and on earth peace among men with whom he is pleased!"* (Lk 2:14)

Jesus came into the world as the Prince of Peace. He brought peace to this weary, disrupted world.

Jesus brings peace to me by teaching me to call God my Father, my Abba. Knowing that I am loved and accepted by the Father is the source of my peace.

Jesus furthermore promised me the Holy Spirit who would make his temple within me. One of the important fruits of the Holy Spirit is peace.

Thank you, Father, Son, and Holy Spirit, for the peace of mind and heart which I enjoy.

9 *"Through the tender mercy of our God, when the day shall dawn upon us from on high to give light to those who sit in darkness and in the shadow of death, to guide our feet into the way of peace."*
(Lk 1:78-79)

How encouraging is the confirmation that Zechariah gives to the prophecies of old—that Jesus would be the source of peace.

Jesus leads me into the "way of peace." He reveals the way I am to follow if I am to attain it.

Lord, "guide my feet into the way of peace," and give me

the courage and strength to commit myself wholeheartedly to that way each day.

10 *Let the peace of Christ rule in your hearts, to which indeed you were called in the one body. And be thankful.* (Col 3:15)

At my baptism I was received as a member into God's family. My loving Father adopted me as his child. Jesus shared his divine life with me, making me a member of his body.

With this dignity I am destined to live at peace with God and with all the members of his family.

Yes, I am truly grateful for this honor. May my life be dedicated to thankfulness.

11 *Rather, speaking the truth in love, we are to grow up in every way into him who is the head, into Christ.* (Eph 4:15)

It is sometimes difficult to be honest, open, and sincere in dealing with others because I myself fear rejection. However, if I "profess the truth in love" I can be objective in speaking about those things which might otherwise create resentment.

As we draw closer to Jesus, then we can deal honestly with others who are also members of his body.

Jesus, you were gentle but honest with others. Help me to pattern my life after yours.

12 *Aspire to live quietly, to mind your own affairs.* (1 Thes 4:11)

How briefly, but how firmly St. Paul tells me to "mind my own business." How right he is!

I am in no position to judge others; only God knows the mind and heart of others. This prerogative belongs to God even though I try so often to assume it myself.

Surely, if I attend to my own affairs I will be at peace. Paul tells me to make this a point of honor.

13 *Therefore, since we are justified by faith, we have peace with God through our Lord Jesus Christ.* (Rom 5:1)

Jesus has made peace with God for me by dying for my sins so that I can be forgiven and healed. By his life, death, and resurrection, Jesus restored me to a rich, personal relationship with the Father, the Holy Spirit, and with himself as my Savior and Redeemer.

This peace which I have from God I should share with others. It helps me rid myself of all grudges, anger, and ill will toward anyone.

Thank you, Jesus, for greeting me so often with your familiar "Peace be with you!"

"eace I leave with you; my peace I give to you; not as the world gives do I give to you. Let not your hearts be troubled, neither let them be afraid." (Jn 14:27)

Jesus came into the world as the Prince of Peace. He came to bring peace to troubled hearts. By his death and resurrection he won that gift for me.

Before ending his earthly sojourn, he promised peace as his special farewell gift to me. As with all his gifts, I must be conditioned and willing to receive it on his terms.

Grant me peace, O Lord.

15 *Peace of God, which passes all understanding, will keep your hearts and your minds in Christ Jesus.* (Phil 4:7)

My heart is so fickle. I become angry or impatient at the slightest provocation. I am so easily threatened. My response to others is frequently a sharp, cutting word.

There is only one remedy: to spend more time with the Lord in prayer so that he can remold my heart.

When my mind and heart are at peace with God, my responses and reaction will reflect his love, peace, and joy. Hasten that day, Lord!

16 *"And I, when I am lifted up from the earth, will draw all men to myself."* (Jn 12:32)

How often I have enjoyed that peace of heart which comes only from the knowledge that all my sins, faults, and failings have been forgiven!

When Jesus was lifted up he nailed my sins to the cross with him. He draws me to himself so that he can fill me with his peace.

Listen to him say: "Peace be with you."

17 *The fruit of the Spirit is love, joy, peace, patience, kindness, goodness, faithfulness.* (Gal 5:22)

When I was baptized, I became the temple of the Holy Spirit. He is present and operative within me, helping me produce his special fruits.

The Holy Spirit is the source of divine love. As I permit the Holy Spirit to mold and transform me, I will become radiant with the peace which only he can give. As Jesus' disciple this is my special mission in life.

18 *"The Lord bless you and keep you: The Lord make his face to shine upon you, and be gracious to you: The Lord lift up his countenance upon you, and give you peace."* (Nm 6:24-26)

This special blessing was dictated by God himself. Its fruits are manifold, but the last in the sequence is peace—God's precious gift of himself.

Lord, grant me the peace which the world cannot give. May I be an instrument of your peace to all you send across my path this day.

19 *"If a house is divided against itself, that house will not be able to stand."* (Mk 3:25)

Peace is a sign of the presence of God, and where God is, there is love. Love is the matrix which binds us together as members of God's family.

On the other hand, sin fragments all interpersonal relationships. Sin is divisive and disruptive, damaging and destructive.

Lord, may I radiate the peace you have given me so that I may become a channel of peace to those with whom I live.

20 *"Peace be with you. As the Father has sent me, even so I send you."* (Jn 20:21)

The knowledge that Jesus loves me so much that he laid down his life for me is the source of genuine peace. He continues to show his forgiving, healing, redeeming love for me personally as I encounter him in the Sacrament of Reconciliation.

Even more, I bring him much joy when I come to him with my sinfulness, because I permit him to be what he wants to be most—Savior and Redeemer.

Such a gift brings deep peace.

21 *[Christ] has now reconciled in his body of flesh by his death, in order to present you holy and blameless and irreproachable before him.* (Col 1:22)

Jesus was delighted to appear to his apostles on the day of the Resurrection to announce to them: "Peace be with you!" His redemptive immolation restored our fractured and fragmented relationship with the Trinity, thus opening the floodgates of peace for all of us.

In the Sacrament of Reconciliation I encounter Jesus personally and privately to hear his reconciling words: "Peace be with you!" This is not an empty greeting, for he fills me with an abundance of his peace.

22 *God has called us to peace.* (1 Cor 7:15)

Peace flows from good relationships. I must first of all be at peace with God by keeping my will in tune with the will of my loving Father.

I must also be at peace with others by respecting them as brothers and sisters in Christ. We all have a common Father in heaven—that makes us a special family.

I must be at peace with myself, accepting myself as I am—with all my gifts and talents, all my limitations and shortcomings, all my faults and failures. I must be happy with myself because God loves me just as I am. Then I will know the peace which this world cannot give.

23 *"I have said this to you, that in me you may have peace."*
(Jn 16:33)

When Jesus called me to be his disciple, he did not promise me a life strewn with fragrant roses. On the contrary, he warned me of the persecution, misunderstanding, and suffering I could expect.

Paradoxically and mysteriously, discipleship will bring peace and joy, because he promised that "in me you will find peace."

24 *Strive for peace with all men, and for the holiness without which no one will see the Lord.* (Heb 12:14)

A community, a family spirit, cannot be built on rules and regulations. It cannot be built on laws. It must be built on love. Love welds us together as brothers and sisters in Christ.

Love compels me to see only the good in others. (That is why we say that love is blind.) Love is also the source of genuine peace.

This is what the psalmist meant when he wrote: "Behold, how good and pleasant it is when brothers dwell in unity!" (Ps 133:1).

25 *For in him all the fulness of God was pleased to dwell, and through him to reconcile to himself all things, whether on earth or in heaven, making peace by the blood of his cross.* (Col 1:19-20)

Sin robs me of my peace. Jesus destroyed the ravages of sin by his death on the cross.

A deep appreciation of his forgiving love will bring me

genuine peace. This was Jesus' first and continual greeting after his resurrection: "Peace be with you."

He greets me daily in the same way.

26 *Let no evil talk come out of your mouths, but only such as is good for edifying, as fits the occasion, that it may impart grace to those who hear.* (Eph 4:29)

A vicious tongue can utterly destroy the peace which should reign among Christians. It devastates that peace which should permeate the family of God.

St. James gives me quite an exhortation about the dangers of the tongue. He compares it to a tiny spark which can set "a great forest ablaze" (Jas 3:5).

On the other hand, "If any one makes no mistakes in what he says he is a perfect man, able to bridle the whole body also" (Jas 3:2).

May my tongue announce peace to everyone I meet.

27 *Let him know that whoever brings back a sinner from the error of his way will save his soul from death and will cover a multitude of sins.* (Jas 5:20)

Sin destroys every vestige of peace. A good relationship with God is the only genuine source of peace. By his death Jesus destroyed sin; hence on the day of the Resurrection he greeted his apostles with "Peace be with you!" (Jn 20:21). If through my prayers, my witnessing, and my encouragement I can bring another person back to God, I will then be a channel of peace to him or her.

As Jesus promised, I, too, will be blessed.

28 *His name will be called ... Prince of Peace. Of the increase of his government and of peace there will be no end.* (Is 9:6-7)

Jesus is rightly called the Prince of Peace because as our Redeemer he reestablished our union with the Father. By his redemptive sacrifice he breached the chasm that separated us from the Father.

He also told me; "No one comes to the Father, but by me" (Jn 14:6).

My personal relationship with the Father is the source of my peace. When I know that the Father loves me, then I can accept myself as I am. Furthermore, I can accept all those persons God sends into my life.

Peace is the exponent of love.

29 *Her* [*wisdom's*] *ways are ways of pleasantness, and all her paths are peace.* (Prv 3:17)

Wisdom teaches me the lifestyle which is in conformity with the will and wishes of my heavenly Father. It helps me recognize that all the eventualities of every day are God's direct or permissive will.

Such wisdom helps me enjoy sunshine or rain, suffering or joy, demanding duties or relaxing moments. Wisdom helps me accept whatever comes, not passively or stoically, but willingly and gladly.

Wisdom's ways are not only pleasant ways—they are the paths which will lead me to peace.

30 *Live in peace, and the God of love and peace will be w...*
(2 Cor 13:11)

When I realize in my heart that I am known and loved by God, when I am aware that I am precious to him, then I can accept myself as I am and I will not be threatened by those I live with. I will see God working in his own mysterious way in every one of them.

With this attitude I will find much peace. That peace is God's gift to me. Moreover, it is his very presence dwelling within me.

31 *For it is the God who said, "Let light shine out of darkness," who has shone in our hearts to give the light of the knowledge of the glory of God in the face of Christ.* (2 Cor 4:6)

Jesus came into the world to bring his peace to every man, woman, and child. He died to gain that peace. Jesus shares that peace with me not only as a personal blessing, but also that I may be a channel of peace to others.

One of the most powerful ways by which I can share that peace is through the radiance of my countenance, the peace and joy of the Lord shining forth in all my thoughts and words, my attitudes and actions.

May my smile ever say, "Peace be with you!"

To Be Persecuted

Blessed are you when men revile you and persecute you and utter all kinds of evil against you falsely on my account.

MATTHEW 5:11

How well Jesus prepared me to become his disciple! He cautioned me about the reception I could expect on earth: "If the world hates you, know that it has hated me before it hated you" (Jn 15:18).

As a struggling disciple I am in good company, for Jesus continues: "they persecuted me, they will persecute you" (v. 20).

A gracious, generous disciple accepts insults, slander, and persecution, not with a self-pitying martyr complex, but rather with the spirit of love which Jesus proposed: "Rejoice and be glad, for your reward is great in heaven" (Mt 5:12). Listening to the wisdom expressed in his Word will condition me and form within me a genuine Christlike attitude under the fire of persecution.

1 *"Blessed are those who are persecuted for righteousness' sake, for theirs is the kingdom of heaven."* (Mt 5:10)

When Jesus called me to follow him and outlined the blueprint for me to follow, he also warned me that I could expect to be misunderstood, criticized, and even persecuted.

The lifestyle which Jesus traced for me may be a red flag to people whose way of life is diametrically opposed to what Jesus asks. They may try to defend themselves by criticizing and persecuting me.

Thank you for warning me, Lord. It helps.

2 *"Remember the word that I said to you, 'A servant is not greater than his master.' If they persecuted me, they will persecute you; if they kept my word, they will keep yours also."* (Jn 15:20)

Jesus knew that I could learn more easily by following in the footsteps of someone who broke ground before me. He taught me not only by outlining a Christian lifestyle, but also by living and experiencing all that I would encounter in my daily life.

Jesus suffered rejection from his birth in Bethlehem until his cruel death on Calvary. He prepares me for the same since I am his friend and disciple.

Jesus, when I am harried, hold on to my hand that I might accept the blows and barbs as silently as you did.

3 *"I have given them thy word; and the world has hated them because they are not of the world, even as I am not of the world."*

(Jn 17:14)

In his powerful high-priestly prayer, Jesus pleaded with his Father for me. He knew that the world would hate me since I am not of the world. How comforting to know that I am not fighting the battle alone. Jesus was rejected and persecuted throughout his whole life on earth. I am certainly in good company.

Knowing the Father's loving concern for me, when persecution comes I can square off my shoulders and forge ahead undaunted.

4 *"Those whom I love, I reprove and chasten; so be zealous and repent. Behold, I stand at the door and knock; if any one hears my voice and opens the door, I will come in to him and eat with him, and he with me."* (Rv 3:19-20)

Jesus calls me to follow him and become his disciple, but I need some conditioning since I find it hard to give myself willingly and entirely to the Lord. Discipline and self-denial, correction and reproof help me to turn my course toward the Lord. What a recompense! Jesus will come to live with me and within me if I open the door on which he is knocking. He does not open the door himself because the latchstring is on the inside.

5 *"You will be hated by all for my name's sake. But not a hair of your head will perish. By your endurance you will gain your lives."* (Lk 21:17-19)

Jesus is reassuring me that nothing will ever happen to me without his knowledge and his permission. Furthermore, he will protect me if I place my trust in him. Moreover, by his own sufferings he has sanctified all the pain which may come my way, that all my sufferings will lead me into heaven and my eternal union with him.

No wonder St. Paul assures me that the sufferings of this life cannot be compared with the glory which awaits me (see Rom 8:18).

6 *"I say to you that hear, Love your enemies, do good to those who hate you, bless those who curse you, pray for those who abuse you."* (Lk 6:27-28)

What an example Jesus gave me as he lived this maxim himself, and while under fire! He healed the ear of Malchus the high priest's servant, in the Garden of Gethsamene; called Judas "friend"; forgave Peter's denial; and pardoned all his disciples for deserting him. He even permitted a thief to steal heaven.

Considering Jesus' own experiences will encourage me to love my enemies.

7 *For the sake of Christ, then, I am content with weaknesses, insults, hardships, persecutions, and calamities; for when I am weak, then I am strong.* (2 Cor 12:10)

Jesus shows me the way. He came into this world weak, vulnerable, dependent. He was rejected and persecuted from the first moment of his earthly sojourn. His real power is love. Love is the most powerful force in all the world. He wanted to elicit from me a loving response.

When I feel persecuted, the Lord says to me as he said to St. Paul: "My grace is sufficient for you, for my power is made perfect in weakness" (2 Cor 12:9).

8 *"But I say to you, Love your enemies and pray for those who persecute you, so that you may be sons of your Father who is in heaven."* (Mt 5:44-45)

One of the worst evils in the world is man's inhumanity to man. The victimizer may not always intend harm or hurt or pain to another. He or she may be suffering from insecurity or from the aftermath of many terrible experiences in life.

When I experience this sort of treatment from another, I can always pray with Jesus: "Father, forgive them; for they know not what they do" (Lk 23:34).

9 *I can will what is right, but I cannot do it. For I do not do the good I want, but the evil I do not want is what I do.* (Rom 7:18-19)

I am not always the persecuted. I may be persecuting others by my lack of sensitivity, my preoccupation with self, or my unwillingness to listen.

Lord, show me how I might have inadvertently wronged others, been insensitive to their needs, or caused their pain.

Father, forgive me, for I do not always know what I do.

10 *"Lord Jesus, receive my spirit."* (Acts 7:59)

St. Stephen's gift of his life to God identifies him with Jesus and his final oblation: "Father, into your hands I commit my spirit" (Lk 23:46). Like Jesus, Stephen was able to make this final gift of himself because this had been the watchword of his entire life.

The more I give, the more I will be able to love. Love will help me accept the little martyrdoms of each day, the little pinpricks which come my way.

"Lord, do not hold this sin against them."

11 *Through many tribulations we must enter the kingdom of God.* (Acts 14:22)

How well St. Paul prepared the early Christians for their lot in life! He had personally experienced suffering and persecution as he tried to live and to proclaim the Good News.

I am no exception. If I am to enter into the reign of God,

the trials and hardships of daily living will help me die to self and surrender more completely to God's plan for me.

I will then see each trial as conditioning—a blessing.

12 *"Blessed are you when men revile you and persecute you and utter all kinds of evil against you falsely on my account."*

(Mt 5:11)

Jesus clearly and unmistakably predicted that if I tried to follow him, I would be persecuted.

Listen to his words: "If you were of the world, the world would love its own; but because you are not of the world, but I chose you out of the world, therefore the world hates you" (Jn 15:19).

Thank you for choosing me, Jesus.

13 *"Rejoice and be glad, for your reward is great in heaven, for so men persecuted the prophets who were before you."*

(Mt 5:12)

What a paradox: to rejoice when I am being persecuted!

The reason is obvious: Jesus was persecuted for proclaiming and living the Good News. He warned that the lot of his followers would be the same.

Since Jesus suffered pain and persecution, he sanctified that suffering for me and made it my stairway into a loving union with him.

14 *The word of the cross is folly to those who are perishing, but to us who are being saved it is the power of God.* (1 Cor 1:18)

The disciples of Jesus could not understand the folly of the cross until after the outpouring of the Holy Spirit. Unfortunately, those who are not open to the influence of the Holy Spirit see the message of the cross as complete absurdity.

Thank you, Lord, for the grace to understand, in a small way, the glory of the cross and the glory awaiting me if I, like you, take up my cross and start toward my own Calvary.

15 *"Whoever would save his life will lose it, and whoever loses his life for my sake will find it."* (Mt 16:25)

So often Jesus seems to speak in riddles and paradoxes, but it only seems so because I am not able to fully understand God's way. Did he not say: "For my thoughts are not your thoughts, neither are your ways my ways" (Is 55:8)?

Jesus, I do understand that you are telling me that life here on earth cannot be compared with life hereafter. Life with you for all eternity is worth any cost here and now. Call it loss and gain!

16 *"In the world you have tribulation; but be of good cheer, I have overcome the world."* (Jn 16:33)

By his passion Jesus not only conquered sin and death, but he gave meaning and efficacy to all the suffering and pain in my life. Pain will always remain in the realm of mystery, but Jesus asks me to trust him. Did he not plead with me: "Let not

your hearts be troubled; believe in God, believe also in me"
(Jn 14:1)?

Jesus, "I believe; help my unbelief!" (Mk 9:24).

17 *And if children, then heirs, heirs of God and fellow heirs with Christ, provided we suffer with him in order that we may also be glorified with him.* (Rom 8:17)

Through his cross Jesus gained for me an eternal heritage.
There is only one requirement for me: I must be willing to
endure suffering and sorrow, pain and persecution along with
Jesus, for in God's mysterious plan, these are steppingstones
into a deeper union with him.

Suffering with Jesus is a small price for so great an inheritance—my glorification with Jesus.

18 *"If the world hates you, know that it has hated me before it hated you."* (Jn 15:18)

I am human enough to want to be accepted as a person, to
be respected for my convictions and my way of life. However,
my lifestyle may prick the conscience of a world which desires
no restrictions and desires to satisfy its every human craving.

I can expect hatred and rejection, but Jesus is my comforter
and consoler, assuring me that since my way of life conforms
with his I should expect the same treatment he received.

19

"Be faithful unto death, and I will give you the crown of life."
(Rv 2:10)

Jesus fell several times along the Way of the Cross, but each time he painfully struggled to his feet and stumbled on toward his destination.

Discouragement can be my greatest obstacle in following the Lord. It is also the favorite tool of the evil one, who tries to wean me away from my determination to live my Christian commitment.

When I stumble or fall, may I hear Jesus say: "Come, follow me!"

20

Far be it from me to glory except in the cross of our Lord Jesus Christ, by which the world has been crucified to me, and I to the world. (Gal 6:14)

To grow in holiness, to mature in Christlikeness, I must keep my focus riveted on Jesus. In doing so, I will always see the shadow of the cross loom up in the background.

At first the cross may frighten me. Then I remember that my worldly pursuits failed to satisfy the hunger of my human heart and often left the ashes of disillusionment in my mouth.

At such moments, I could often see Jesus beckoning me to the absurdity of the cross. In the company of Jesus and in the shadow of his cross I begin to see the "glory of the cross."

21 *Rejoice in so far as you share Christ's sufferings, that you may also rejoice and be glad when his glory is revealed.* (1 Pt 4:13)

Like his Master, Peter encourages me to rejoice in all the persecutions, insults, misunderstandings, hardships, and sufferings which may come my way. I can be certain that not only will Jesus empower me to endure them, but the Holy Spirit will fill me with his peace and joy.

My joyful acceptance of this type of suffering can also be my special mission in life.

22 *If you are reproached for the name of Christ, you are blessed, because the spirit of glory and of God rests upon you.*
(1 Pt 4:14)

Life is such a paradox! Losing life, I gain life; being poor, I become rich.

Discipline, self-denial, and detachment are all foreign to the human heart. Thanks to the light of the Holy Spirit, the absurdity of the cross and persecution become the way of perfection for me.

Come, Holy Spirit, continue to light my way.

23 *May you be strengthened with all power, according to his glorious might, for all endurance and patience with joy, giving thanks to the Father, who has qualified us to share in the inheritance of the saints in light.* (Col 1:11-12)

I can always depend on the fidelity of Jesus. He promised: "I will not leave you orphaned; I will come back to you" (Jn 14:18).

His presence endows me with the strength I need to meet the problems of each day. His presence brings joy in adversity.

Above all, his presence makes me a member of his Body, along with the angels and saints.

Come what may, I give thanks to my Father in heaven.

24 *Blessed is the man who endures trial, for when he has stood the test he will receive the crown of life which God has promised to those who love him.* (Jas 1:12)

This is a special beatitude to encourage me in times of suffering. I react in many different ways in trials and tribulations. At times I am tempted to feel sorry for myself. I may get angry and impatient. I have a tendency to grow bitter when suffering seems unjust.

I can patiently bear affliction only if I love. Suffering is a sign of God's love for me. Jesus asks me if I love enough to carry a little portion of his cross. Can I refuse?

25 *I consider that the sufferings of this present time are not worth comparing with the glory that is to be revealed to us.* (Rom 8:18)

What a compelling example Jesus gave me when he was transfigured on Mount Tabor! The splendor of his divinity burst forth from his humanity to assure me that this is the splendor of the life he will share with me after the trials and tribulations of my earthly sojourn are ended.

Jesus knew that his followers would be scandalized when he voluntarily laid down his life. I need this reassurance of the glory which awaits me.

"Lord, it is good for me to be here."

26 *"This is the stone which was rejected by you builders, but which has become the head of the corner."* (Acts 4:11)

Jesus is the building stone rejected by those who did not recognize him. Yet God's ways are not our ways. In God's divine plan Jesus became the very cornerstone of God's kingdom.

As a follower of Jesus my lifestyle may not conform to the mentality of some of my friends and acquaintances. I may be invited less frequently to their gatherings, or maybe not at all. When this happens I have the assurance that my relationship with the heavenly court is deepening.

27 *Even if you do suffer for righteousness' sake, you will be blessed. Have no fear of them, nor be troubled.* (1 Pt 3:14)

Jesus did not promise me a royal, garland-strewn road to heaven. All he offered me was his own way of the cross, but with the assurance that he would not leave me. He will be with me to shoulder most of the burden.

When I am persecuted, I am walking more closely in the footsteps of Jesus. This path will lead me to the glory he has prepared for me.

Keep me going, Lord.

28 *Indeed all who desire to live a godly life in Christ Jesus will be persecuted.* (2 Tm 3:12)

Persecution is a sure sign that I am walking in the way Jesus mapped out for me. Jesus tried to prepare me for persecution:

"If they persecuted me, they will persecute you" (Jn 15:20).

The persecutions which are rampant today are subtle: raised eyebrows at certain standards of morality, ridicule for bringing another child into the world, materialistic standards of success, and so on.

Lord, you told me to rejoice and be glad when persecutions come. I am counting on your help to recognize them and to handle them your way.

29 *In my flesh I complete what is lacking in Christ's afflictions for the sake of his body, that is, the church.* (Col 1:24)

The body of Jesus is suffering unmercifully in the world today because of the injustice, the cruelty, the avarice, the selfishness of those who do not know Jesus or his infinite love for them.

Suffering and persecution will help me sympathize with the suffering members of Christ's body. My compassion should motivate me to alleviate whatever suffering I can.

"Truly, I say to you, as you did it to one of the least of these my brethren, you did it to me" (Mt 25:40).

30 *"And as Moses lifted up the serpent in the wilderness, so must the Son of man be lifted up, that whoever believes in him may have eternal life."* (Jn 3:14-15)

As I drive through the city or along a country road, the crosses high on the steeples of the churches are a constant reminder to me that God so loved me that he gave me his Son as my Redeemer.

Jesus promised that if he were lifted up, he would draw all men to himself.

I try to say "thank you" each time I see a cross. It is a traffic sign assuring me I am on the right road toward my eternal destiny.

31 *The word of the cross is folly to those who are perishing, but to us who are being saved it is the power of God.* (1 Cor 1:18)

I cannot understand the folly of the cross. My whole human nature shrinks from the pain which the cross represents, yet I find a magnetic attraction to the cross.

How often I want to come and rest in the shadow of the cross! When I am insulted or persecuted, slandered or misunderstood, hurt or wronged, I find great peace and consolation as I approach the cross.

In the shadow of the cross of Jesus my own cross becomes tolerable. It leads me into a more generous commitment as his disciple.

Part III
The Commitment

Commitment

I have come to do thy will, O God.

C ommitment is the third stage in becoming a full-fledged
disciple of the Lord. Commitment is a direction of will—
a desire and determination to give *all* without counting the cost.

Commitment is the maturing stage of our spiritual growth.
To seek holiness means to follow Jesus with the same mind-set
he had in giving himself completely to his redemptive mission.

Discipleship requires the total gift of self. Anyone who
holds back anything of himself or herself, or clings to anything
in this world, does not yet have that fully responsive and open
heart which is essential for discipleship.

Commitment is dying to self and to the world; it is a matter
of priority. God must be number one on our priorities—he
must be our sole priority. Everything follows from this.

Love is the motivating power which makes total dedication
possible. Loving and serving God "with all your heart, and
with all your soul, and with all your strength, and with all your
mind" will enable us to make an unconditional, total, and
ongoing commitment (Lk 10:27).

The following scriptural passages have been selected to guide
us into a deeper, more dedicated commitment. May God's
Word make us stronger in our resolve and enrich our lives.

Prayer of Abandonment

Father, I abandon myself into your hands;
Do with me as you will.
For whatever you do I thank you.
I am ready for all, I accept all.
Let only your will be done in me,
as in all your creatures.
I ask nothing else, my Lord.
Into your hands I commend my soul;
I give it to you with the love of my heart,
for I love you and so need to give myself—
to surrender myself into your hands
with a trust beyond all measure,
because you are my Father.

Brother Charles of Jesus

To Commitment

Did you not know that I must be busy with my Father's affairs?
LUKE 2:49, JB

Jesus is the way. He is our exemplar. We can be certain that he does not ask us to endure everything which he himself has not experienced.

Jesus was single-hearted in his dedication and determination to do his Father's will at all times.

In the sacred precincts at the temple at the age of twelve, Jesus revealed his dedication when he explained to Joseph and Mary why he remained behind: "Did you not know that I must be in my Father's house?" (Lk 2:49). This single-heartedness was repeated many times throughout his earthly sojourn.

From the dark, cavernous gloom of Gethsemane we hear his acquiescence, "Father, if thou art willing, remove this cup from me; nevertheless not my will, but thine, be done" (Lk 22:42). His total and final oblation echoes above the satanic din of Calvary, "Father, into thy hands I commit my spirit!" (Lk 23:46). Jesus rose from the dead that he might live with us and within us, disposing and enabling us to make our commitment to the Father.

1 *By faith Abraham obeyed when he was called to go out to a place which he was to receive as an inheritance; and he went out, not knowing where he was to go.* (Heb 11:8)

Abraham is called the Father of Faith. Certainly he deserved this title, because he was only gradually drawn to know the one true God. He left family and friends to journey to a strange land.

God has given me so many proofs of his loving providence. How much more willing should I be to respond to his invitation to commit myself totally to his plans for me, even though he leads me in strange ways.

Father Abraham, help me to say yes.

2 *"Take your son, your only son Isaac, whom you love, and go to the land of Mori'ah, and offer him there as a burnt offering upon one of the mountains of which I shall tell you."* (Gn 22:2)

God's test of Abraham's faith was extreme. Human sacrifice was common, yet to sacrifice his only son—on whom God's promise of posterity depended—seemed preposterous.

Abraham's heart must have been broken, but he did not renege on his commitment.

As I ponder Abraham's great faith and his unselfish generosity I find much incentive to carry out my mini-commitments.

3 *By faith he [Moses] left Egypt, not being afraid of the anger of the king; for he endured as seeing him who is invisible.* (Heb 11:27)

What a shining example of total commitment Moses gave me. He turned his back on all the pleasures of Pharaoh's court. "Choosing rather to share ill-treatment with the people of God than to enjoy the fleeting pleasures of sin" (Heb 11:25).

If I am able to keep the "invisible God" in mind and heart throughout the day, I will be better able to daily surrender myself to him in love. When I become fearful and hesitant in giving myself, Jesus says to me: "It is I; do not be afraid" (Jn 6:20).

4 *Jesus Christ ... was not Yes and No; but in him it is always Yes.* (2 Cor 1:19)

Jesus committed himself to his mission without any reservation. From his first breath in Bethlehem to his last labored gasp on the cross, he gave himself totally to the Father's will.

Jesus himself reminds me of his commitment to the Father's plan of salvation. "For I have come down from heaven, not to do my own will, but the will of him who sent me" (Jn 6:38).

With Jesus at my side, I will examine my own commitment.

5 *"You shall not tempt the Lord your God."* (Mt 4:7)

One of my frequent temptations is to question God's ways. Why did the Lord let this happen? If God is so good, why all this suffering? The list of questions is endless.

In my pride I try to play God. I flatter myself by thinking

that I know better than God what is good for me.

Humility is saying "yes" to God's divine designs for me. In the Garden of Gethsemane Jesus gave me the example: "Father, if thou art willing, remove this cup from me; nevertheless not my will, but thine, be done" (Lk 22:42).

6 *"Man shall not live by bread alone, but by every word that proceeds from the mouth of God."* (Mt 4:4)

Jesus successfully repelled Satan and recommitted himself to his mission. Jesus assures me that God's Word will always be the source of my victory over temptation.

His Word will be the source of enlightenment and discernment. It will give me hope and encouragement. It will provide me with strength, courage, and perseverance.

Lord, may I be fed daily at the table of your Word.

7 *"You shall worship the Lord your God and him only shall you serve."* (Mt 4:10)

Amid all the temptations, allurements, enticements of power, wealth, recognition, and influence, I must keep my attention fixed on my first priority: my loving Father and all that will bring me closer to him. Jesus stated it so clearly for me.

I can even be deceived by a "do-gooder" attitude, cultivated for my own gratification and not for the love of the Lord and my fellow man.

Thank you, Jesus, for showing me the way when you were tempted in the desert.

8 *"I, when I am lifted up from the earth, will draw all men to myself."* (Jn 12:32)

The cross is a symbol of total commitment. It speaks to me of my own commitment. Jesus persevered to the end even though it meant "death on a cross!" (Phil 2:8).

The cross of Jesus has a drawing power, as he foretold. I see the cross displayed many times throughout the course of each day. It reminds me of my commitment.

I want to commit myself in faith to consent, to trust, to abandon myself with an all-out willingness to do what pleases the Father.

Jesus, I need your support. Keep assuring me of your presence and power.

9 *"Father, into thy hands I commit my spirit!"* (Lk 23:46)

The experience of having fulfilled his Father's will to the very letter must have been a source of great comfort and consolation to Jesus as he handed himself over in death.

As I strive to do what my loving Father asks of me, I might experience some pain. The sacrifice may seem too great. Nevertheless, the satisfaction which comes to me in accepting what God asks will be a tremendous reward in itself.

Love must give and giving brings untold joy.

10 *"It is finished."* (Jn 19:30)

This is Jesus' final and total gift of himself to his Father for me. He fulfilled perfectly his commitment.

Jesus must have found great peace in the fact that he proved his boundless love for me. He could give no more. The proof of his love is beyond question.

Again I am reminded of his words the night before his death: "Greater love has no man than this, that a man lay down his life for his friends" (Jn 15:13).

Love asks for a response. Limitless love requires a limitless response. Can I fail to give unstintingly?

11 *"Let us also go, that we may die with him."* (Jn 11:16)

Perhaps St. Thomas was not aware of the significance of his advice to me. I must walk with Jesus, travel with him ever at my side, die with him by dying to myself in dozens of little ways each day.

This is the only way I can become a true disciple of Jesus. Jesus mapped out this way very clearly in his Word.

Jesus, give me a receptive heart to receive your Word that I may bring forth fruit in patience.

12 *Consider Jesus, the apostle and high priest of our confession. He was faithful to him who appointed him.* (Heb 3:1-2)

When I fix my eyes on a goal, I am automatically drawn in

that direction and become less aware of the many distracting and disturbing objects cluttering my path.

Likewise, when I reflect on the faithfulness of Jesus, who never wavered in his total commitment, I am drawn into greater generosity.

Keeping my gaze on Jesus also helps me bridge those discouraging moments and strengthens my resolve to persevere as he did.

13 *"Behold, I am the handmaid of the Lord; let it be to me according to your word."* (Lk 1:38)

Mary was the perfect disciple of Jesus. Mary heard the angel's invitation, then made her total commitment to the Lord.

Jesus explained that his Mother's true greatness was the fact that she had heard the Word of God and kept it (see Lk 11:28).

Listening to God's Word and trying to live it in my own life will make me a disciple of Jesus. Like Mary, my motivating power must be love.

14 *"Blessed is she who believed that there would be a fulfilment of what was spoken to her from the Lord."* (Lk 1:45)

Mary was asked to fulfill a role which according to human standards was impossible. Yet without hesitation she accepted her call. I am blest because of her trust in the Lord.

My loving Father calls me to a specific role. The task at hand may seem virtually impossible, yet with him I can do all things, if I only trust him.

Mary, be a patient Mother to me and take me by the hand when I begin to falter.

15 *Standing by the cross of Jesus [was] his mother.* (Jn 19:25)

In so many ways Mary is the model and exemplar for the dedicated disciple of Jesus. What pathos in John's brief statement: "Standing by the cross of Jesus [was] his mother."

Mary's posture was one of total dedication and oblation even to the point of death. The razor-sharp sword of sorrow must have been excruciating, yet she did not flinch one iota in her commitment.

May my courage and commitment be spawned by that same love.

16 *"The Son of man also came not to be served but to serve, and to give his life as a ransom for many."* (Mk 10:45)

Jesus called me to follow him. Now he is waiting for my commitment. Again Jesus showed me the way. He came into the world to give me an example of commitment. He did not come to be served, but to serve. No task was too humiliating. He even washed the feet of the apostles before the Last Supper, and encourages me to do the same. "If I ... have washed your feet, you also ought to wash one another's feet" (Jn 13:14).

Jesus' commitment was so total that he laid down his life to rescue me from the clutches of sin and death. Can I refuse to serve?

17 *"Not every one who says to me, 'Lord, Lord,' shall enter the kingdom of heaven, but he who does the will of my Father who is in heaven."* (Mt 7:21)

Jesus looks only at my heart. Words piously uttered are not magical formulas guaranteeing good fruits. External acts of worship can be mere formalism unless they spring from a loving heart.

Jesus asks me to keep my will running parallel with the Father's will and not perpendicular to it. My "yes" to the Father, arising from and stabilized by love, is a commitment pleasing to my Father.

18 *"If you are offering your gift at the altar, and there remember that your brother has something against you, leave your gift there before the altar and go; first be reconciled to your brother, and then come and offer your gift."* (Mt 5:23-24)

If I want to commit myself to follow Jesus, I must strive to have the heart and mind which he reflected in his attitudes and relationships. Jesus reached out in loving forgiveness even when his enemies vented diabolical hatred against him. "Father, forgive them" (Lk 23:34).

Anger endangers my relationships with others. It disturbs my peace of mind and makes prayer impossible. Jesus' directives and example are basic to my discipleship.

19 *"No one can serve two masters; for either he will hate the one and love the other, or he will be devoted to the one and despise the other. You cannot serve God and mammon."* (Mt 6:24)

To be a disciple I must make a full-time commitment. I must belong to Jesus completely. "No one can serve two masters." My commitment is ongoing. I must be willing to mature. Mary's fiat embraced her whole life, though she did not understand all that she was saying yes to at the Annunciation.

Lord, keep your help coming my way so that I can say yes regardless of what you ask.

20 *"No one who puts his hand to the plow and looks back is fit for the kingdom of God."* (Lk 9:62)

To plow a straight furrow a person must keep looking ahead. If I want to commit my life to following Jesus, I, too, must look ahead. I must keep my gaze fixed on Jesus; then all the mundane concerns around me will fall into perspective.

Jesus shows me the way by pointing to his own lifestyle, especially the outpouring of his love upon everyone who comes to him. He epitomizes the way of life for me when he says:

"Love one another; even as I have loved you, that you also love one another" (Jn 13:34). How straight is the furrow I am plowing?

21 *"Truly, truly, I say to you, unless a grain of wheat falls into the earth and dies, it remains alone; but if it dies, it bears much fruit."* (Jn 12:24)

How vividly Jesus outlined the total commitment expected of his followers! The pastoral image of a grain of wheat dying to produce a rich harvest speaks forcefully of total giving.

At first the price might seem too great, but love will help me see the great privilege which is mine. Love will not be satisfied until it gives generously of itself.

Jesus, you told me that in losing my life I would gain life. Enkindle in my heart the burning love which will propel me into action.

22 *"Behold, Lord, the half of my goods I give to the poor; and if I have defrauded any one of anything, I restore it fourfold."*
(Lk 19:8)

Jesus reached out in the healing love of acceptance and friendship to Zacchaeus. Instantly a great transformation took place within him. Touched by the love of Jesus for him, Zacchaeus made a very generous commitment.

As I come to listen to Jesus, I grow to know him better. The better I know him, the more I will love him. Only when I love him will I be able to make a true commitment and remain faithful to it. Stay with me, Lord, as my guest, that I may always be aware of your love.

23 *"Lord, you know everything; you know that I love you."* (Jn 21:17)

Three times Jesus asked Peter if he loved him. Jesus wanted to emphasize to Peter that he could not make any commitment to feed the flock unless he loved and loved deeply. History shows that Peter proved that love.

I cannot be a disciple of Jesus until I have experienced his love for me to such an extent that I want to commit myself totally to him.

This kind of giving is the source of much joy.

24 *"By this all men will know that you are my disciples, if you have love for one another."* (Jn 13:35)

The test of discipleship is not what I accomplish for the Lord, or how much good I am able to do for others, but rather how much I love.

To be a true disciple I must love as much as Jesus loved both friend and foe. He could say of himself: "Greater love has no man than this, that a man lay down his life for his friends" (Jn 15:13). Or again: "As the Father has loved me, so I have loved you" (Jn 15:9).

The depth of commitment depends upon how much I love.

25 *Let us also lay aside every weight, and sin which clings so closely, and let us run with perseverance the race that is set before us, looking to Jesus the pioneer and perfecter of our faith.* (Heb 12:1-3)

Jesus is the architect of this new way of life. He not only taught me how to live his way, but he lived it himself. He had to endure the cross before receiving the glory of his triumph. He was faithful to the end, "obedient unto death, even death on a cross" (Phil 2:8).

I am to follow him. When I get discouraged, he reminds me: "I am with you always, to the close of the age" (Mt 28:20).

"Consider him who endured from sinners such hostility against himself, so that you may not grow weary or fainthearted" (Heb 12:3).

26 *Have this mind among yourselves, which is yours in Christ Jesus, who ... emptied himself, taking the form of a servant.* (Phil 2:5, 7)

Jesus emptied himself of everything for my salvation. He gave up his Mother. He had nowhere to lay his head. He even gave up his own will, that he might be in tune with his Father's will at all times. He came "to give his life as a ransom for many" (Mt 20:28).

Can I be a true disciple if I cling to my petty little attachments? Lord, give me that spirit of detachment and generosity which will enable me to empty myself more and more each day.

27 *Rejoice always, pray constantly, give thanks in all circum-stances; for this is the will of God in Christ Jesus for you.*
(1 Thes 5:16-18)

This scriptural admonition spells out clearly the road that I, as a disciple, must travel to spread joy in a confused, fearful, wounded world.

To accomplish this, I must spend time in prayer—resting, relaxing, and basking in the sunshine of God's presence, and I must "pray constantly."

As I ponder God's goodness to me and to all people I am overwhelmed, and my heart sings his praises in thanking him constantly.

This is my commitment.

28 *"You shall love the Lord your God with all your heart, and with all your soul, and with all your strength, and with all your mind."* (Lk 10:27)

Discipleship means a total gift of self. To be a disciple I must love with all my heart, mind, and soul. Unless I love the Lord, I cannot give myself to him totally and unconditionally.

On the other hand, once I have experienced his tender love for me, I cannot help but give myself to him without reser-vation.

Then I can honestly say: "I have come to do thy will, O God" (Heb 10:7).

29 *"This joy of mine is now full. He must increase, but I must decrease."* (Jn 3:29-30)

My spiritual growth consists in dying more to self and permitting God's divine life to fill, transform, and unite me with himself.

As I decrease, he can increase within me. The psalmist expresses this truth so poetically: "Nevertheless I am continually with thee; thou dost hold my right hand. Thou dost guide me with thy counsel, and afterward thou wilt receive me to glory. Whom have I in heaven but thee? And there is nothing upon earth that I desire besides thee." (Ps 73:23-25)

30 *"Do this in remembrance of me."* (Lk 22:19)

Jesus' request is brief, but imperative. The Eucharist sums up Jesus' total oblation and immolation to the Father. He invites me to unite the gift of myself to his oblation so that he can present it to the Father for me.

Jesus asks me to make my offering regularly and repeatedly, thus fulfilling this prophecy: "From the rising of the sun to its setting my name is great among the nations, and in every place incense is offered to my name, and a pure offering" (Mal 1:11).

Jesus, you became Eucharist for me. As your disciple let me become Eucharist to others.

31 *"Go therefore and make disciples of all nations."* (Mt 28:19)

A disciple is a person who loves and knows without a doubt that he is loved by God. When I have experienced Jesus' love for me, I want everyone to experience that same love. This is what Jesus meant when he asked me to "make disciples of all nations."

I can make disciples not so much by preaching, but rather by radiating the love of God which has been poured into my heart by the Holy Spirit who has been given to me (see Rom 5:5).

Lord, may I be a humble witness to your would-be disciples.

To Love

Abide in my love.

JOHN 15:9

J esus came into the world to reveal the boundless love of the Father for us and also to manifest his own love.

He proved that there is no greater love than his by laying down his life for us.

He also poured into our hearts the Holy Spirit, who is the very source of love.

Once we have experienced his love for us, we cannot help but be his disciples.

As we pray with his Word in this chapter we will find ourselves responding more graciously and more generously to his overwhelming love. Then we will be true disciples because Jesus himself said: "By this all men will know that you are my disciples, if you have love for one another" (Jn 13:35).

1 *"For God so loved the world that he gave his only Son."* (Jn 3:16)

God so loved me that he gave me the greatest possible gift—the gift of himself in the person of Jesus, my Redeemer. If I were the only person alive, he still would have given me the gift of himself for my salvation.

When I respond generously to this gift, his love and mine will reach its fulfillment: my total and eternal union with him.

Lord, you continue to baffle me by the mystery of your love.

2 *He who does not love does not know God; for God is love.* (1 Jn 4:8)

I cannot love God unless I know him, and I cannot know him unless I have listened to him. To know God experientially and to be aware of his abiding love, I must regularly spend time being with him, basking in his presence, and prayerfully listening to him with all my heart.

Only by meeting the Lord each day in prayer will I get to know him as a loving, gracious God, and only then will I be able to establish a personal relationship with him.

Lord, fill me with your love.

3 *"Because you are precious in my eyes, and honored, and I love you."* (Is 43:4)

Repeatedly my Father expresses his love for me. How I need to hear these words over and over again! When I reflect on my self-centeredness, my pride, the ulterior motives which prompt me into action, I find myself very unlovable.

As I listen with all my heart to the tender words of my heavenly Father telling me that I am precious in his eyes, then I know I am lovable, and I can more easily accept myself for what I am.

Thank you, Father, for loving me just as I am.

4 *"You shall love your neighbor as yourself."* (Mt 22:39)

By his own example Jesus taught me how to love. He gradually led me to different levels of love. To love my neighbor as myself is the first level.

Only when I know that God loves me so much that he adopted me as his child will I be able to love others. If I am his adopted son or daughter, then my neighbor is God's child also, and therefore my brother or my sister.

Jesus, teach me how to love.

5 *"Truly, I say to you, as you did it to one of the least of these my brethren, you did it to me."* (Mt 25:40)

When Jesus leads me to this second level of love, he is really saying, "Love your neighbor as you love me," because what I do for my neighbor I do for Jesus himself.

Jesus is also speaking here about the ordinary, overt, positive works of love which are at my disposal every day.

Jesus, help me to see you in my neighbor.

6 *"A new commandment I give to you, that you love one another; even as I have loved you, that you also love one another."*
(Jn 13:34)

In leading me to this third level of love, Jesus is pointing to his own example. His love for me is so great that he laid down his life for me.

In love he asks me to accept the little pinpricks of each day, the difficult duties, the little misunderstandings, the inconveniences of daily living, and so on.

Notice, too, that Jesus set forth this level of love at the Last Supper as his final will and testament. This adds greater urgency to his request.

7 *"That they may all be one; even as thou, Father, art in me, and I in thee, that they also may be in us, so that the world may believe that thou hast sent me."* (Jn 17:21)

Love seeks union—oneness. This fourth level of love is the adhesive which binds us together in deep personal relationships.

Jesus loves me so much that he shares his divine life with me. He prays that I may love enough to allow him to establish that same bond of love between all the members of his family, that we might be one body with him.

What a witness to a weary world!

8 *"I have loved you with an everlasting love; therefore I have continued my faithfulness to you."* (Jer 31:3)

I am so fickle, so forgetful. In my self-will I walk my own way. How often I am carried off on a tangent—away from my fundamental desire to love my Lord!

Even so, when I listen with all my heart, I can hear my Father say: "I love you anyway. I love you with an age-old love, and it will never change because I am God and not man."

Thank you for loving me, Lord, and I love you too!

9 *In this is love, not that we loved God but that he loved us and sent his Son to be the expiation for our sins.* (1 Jn 4:10)

It is difficult for me to fathom this truth: that God first loved me. I must keep reminding myself that I would not be enjoying my gifted life if he had not loved me before I could even respond to his love.

Somehow I feel I must earn God's love, I must merit it. But that is impossible. All that God asks of me is to let him love me just as I am.

It is only when I experience his love for me that I am able to respond in love to him, and to others.

10 *Whatever your task, work heartily, as serving the Lord and not men.* (Col 3:23)

What I do in life is not nearly as important as *why* I do it. If my attitude is the same as Jesus', then I will give everything I do as the gift of myself to the Father.

This resolve intensifies my motivation and brings me greater satisfaction.

11 *"My steadfast love shall not depart from you."* (Is 54:10)

I get rather discouraged at times, especially when I resolve to love God more faithfully and serve my neighbor more graciously, only to find that I fail again and again. My self-centeredness wins the day so often. At times I doubt whether or not God can really love me as I am.

What hope and encouragement I receive when I hear God assuring me that he loves me just as I am, and that his love shall never leave me!

How fortunate I am to be one of his adopted children!

12 *"If a man loves me, he will keep my word, and my Father will love him, and we will come to him and make our home with him."* (Jn 14:23)

When I love a person I enjoy being in that person's company, mutually sharing our joys and sorrows.

Jesus promised that if I am willing to receive his love, he and his Father will make their dwelling place with me and within me.

He is truly Emmanuel—God with me.

"Stay with us, for it is toward evening and the day is now far spent" (Lk 24:29).

13 *Whatever you do, in word or deed, do everything in the name of the Lord Jesus, giving thanks to God the Father through him.* (Col 3:17)

If my focus is always on Jesus, then I will be forming habitual patterns of living which will be in conformity with the mind of Christ.

This attitude will naturally be reflected in my speech and actions, and it will give glory to God.

"Put on the new nature, created after the likeness of God" (Eph 4:24).

14 *"By this all men will know that you are my disciples, if you have love for one another."* (Jn 13:35)

It was said of the early Christians: "See how they love one another."

Jesus made the love of neighbor the badge of discipleship. By my loving concern for others I can witness to the fact that I am a follower of Jesus.

Furthermore, by permitting his love to radiate through me, I can bring many others to know and love the Lord. In turn, they, too, will become more loving in their own apostolates.

This is what it means to be a disciple.

15 *"I know the plans I have for you," says the Lord, "plans for welfare and not for evil, to give you a future and a hope."*
(Jer 29:11)

Even before I was born, my Father had plans for my welfare. He laid out every detail of my life for me to achieve happiness. How often I let fear, worry, and anxiety rob me of peace when problems loom up in my life!

Lord, help me to recognize that every apparent failure, every reversal is only another steppingstone into a deeper union with you.

16 *There is no fear in love, but perfect love casts out fear.*
(1 Jn 4:18)

The reason I have so many fears and feel so insecure is that I am not always aware of the great love which God has for me.

My primary fear is that I have sinned and may have incurred God's disfavor. But as I begin to comprehend God's forgiving, healing love, Jesus' eagerness to be my Savior and Redeemer, my fears begin to vanish.

As my love becomes more perfect, it will cast out all fear. Jesus, hasten that day!

17 *Give thanks to the Lord, for he is good, for his steadfast love endures for ever.* (Ps 136)

This refrain is repeated twenty-six times in this psalm. This repetition transforms my heart and helps me form the habit of being aware of his merciful, compassionate love, regardless of what I have done.

Yes, Lord, what comfort and consolation, what hope and encouragement your enduring, merciful love brings to me! Thank you for loving me.

18 *But God, who is rich in mercy, out of the great love with which he loved us, even when we were dead through our trespasses, made us alive together with Christ (by grace you have been saved).*
(Eph 2:4-5)

Jesus fulfilled all the Old Testament promises of God's forgiving love. St. Paul reminds us of this fulfillment throughout his writings.

Only love can forgive. Jesus not only freed me from my brokenness, but he also remains with me to share the ups and downs of my daily living.

My resurrection has already begun. Alleluia!

19 *"Greater love has no man than this, that a man lay down his life for his friends."* (Jn 15:13)

Jesus not only made this extravagant statement but he proved it by freely giving up his life for my salvation. Did he not say: "I lay down my life.... No one takes it from me; but I lay it down of my own accord" (Jn 10:17-18)?

Why do I fear? Why do I hesitate? I am lovable and I am loved. Jesus will love me right into heaven with him. "Perfect love casts out fear" (1 Jn 4:18).

20 *"When you pass through the waters I will be with you; and through the rivers, they shall not overwhelm you; when you walk through fire you shall not be burned, and the flame shall not consume you."* (Is 43:2)

My Father's protective love overwhelms me at every moment of the day. When the waters of trial and tribulation and the fire of temptation assail me, I know his love will always rescue me. His strong arms will shield me from all danger.

His words are almost audible: "Fear not—trust me."

With all my heart I want to say: "Yes, Father, I do trust you always and everywhere."

21 *Walk in love, as Christ loved us and gave himself up for us, a fragrant offering and sacrifice to God.* (Eph 5:2)

Love by its very nature must give. If all my actions are motivated by love, then I will want to offer everything I do to the Father.

In the Eucharistic celebration I have the privilege of presenting my love, expressed by all the thoughts, words, and deeds I perform, to my Father through Jesus, my eternal high priest.

May my gift be a pleasing fragrance to you, O Lord.

22 *Cast all your anxieties on him, for he cares about you.* (1 Pt 5:7)

What a touching sight to see a little child nestled in the loving arms of his father! The child entrusts himself to his father because he realizes that his father loves him.

Should I not have even greater trust and confidence in my heavenly Father? I need to listen often to the inspired words of St. John: "There is no fear in love, but perfect love casts out fear" (1 Jn 4:18).

23 *"I, I am He who blots out your transgressions for my own sake, and I will not remember your sins."* (Is 43:25)

These words of the Lord reveal his boundless love for me. Love must be translated into action. Divine love gives beyond all my human comprehension.

God wants to forgive me more than I could ever want to be forgiven. His infinite love compels him to wipe out my offenses and never to remember my sinfulness.

Thank you, Lord, for this reassurance of your tender love.

24 *By this we know love, that he laid down his life for us; and we ought to lay down our lives for the brethren.* (1 Jn 3:16)

Jesus proved that there is no greater love than to lay down one's life for one's friends. As his dying wish he pleaded with me: "Love one another as I have loved you" (Jn 15:12).

My love for God is gauged by my love for my neighbor. Even though my love may never be tested by martyrdom, it will be tested by the many little opportunities to do a kind deed which present themselves each day.

Lord, accept every act of love as done for you alone.

25 *God shows his love for us in that while we were yet sinners Christ died for us.* (Rom 5:8)

Somehow I feel unworthy of God's love for me. I have the inherent feeling that I must deserve or earn his love.

How plainly John teaches: "In this is love, not that we loved God but that he loved us" (1 Jn 4:10).

Furthermore, God so loved me that he gave me his own divine Son. Thank you, Lord.

26 *Grace and truth came through Jesus Christ.* (Jn 1:17)

God loves me with an enduring love. It is immutable. His love never changes, regardless of what I have done.

How frightening it is to realize that I have "control" over God's love for me! I can be open to receiving his love, or I can refuse to expose myself totally to it. I may fear that he will ask too much of me.

Jesus, may your boundless love find a home in my heart.

27 *"I have swept away your transgressions like a cloud, and your sins like mist; return to me, for I have redeemed you."*
(Is 44:22)

A fleecy cloud can be wisked away by a gentle breeze. A mist disappears quickly with the warm rays of the rising sun.

With this beautiful image, my compassionate Father portrays his merciful love. His love obliterates my sinfulness as he bathes me in the sunshine of his love.

Only one condition is required: "Return to me"—which is another way of saying, "Be open to receiving my love."

28 *From his fulness have we all received, grace upon grace.* (Jn 1:16)

The endless manifestation of the Father's love for me is found in the gift of his Son, Jesus, to me. Jesus, in turn, revealed his love by giving up his life's blood on the cross.

The Holy Spirit continues the flow of divine love into me by his indwelling, the very source of love.

Jesus, how could I doubt that I am loved? How could I fear that I may be unlovable?

29 *See what love the Father has given us, that we should be called children of God; and so we are.* (1 Jn 3:1)

I am proud of my good parents and my lineage. Yet these roots are transitory. I have an even greater dignity: I belong to the family of God. I am his adopted child for all eternity. What greater proof do I need to know how much God loves me?

Aware of my true dignity, I can respond more wholeheartedly to God's boundless love by adopting the lifestyle of a true disciple.

30 *The Father himself loves you, because you have loved me and have believed that I came from the Father.* (Jn 16:27)

The Father loves me so much he called me into existence and invited me to become a member of his family through baptism. He continues to pour his love into me by the Holy Spirit who has been given to me.

Jesus tells me that he loves me as much as the Father loves him—that is, with an infinite love.

Such love compels me to respond with all the love of my heart.

31 *"As the Father has loved me, so have I loved you; abide in my love."* (Jn 15:9)

These earthshaking words must register high on the Richter scale! The Father loves Jesus with an infinite love. Jesus, in turn, assures me that he loves me with the same infinite love.

Then he encourages me to bask in the sunshine of his love, to permit him to nourish, warm, and cheer me. Yes, the sunshine of his love may even tan me, that I may glow with his love and reflect it to others.

Words fail me, but my heart responds: "I love you, too, Jesus."